Childhood Memories
of the
Great Depression Era

**Stories
as seen through the eyes
of a
nine-year old boy
in
the year 1931**

Ted A. Woodworth

Author of *The Black Walnut Farm Series*

**Emerald Ink Publishing
Hot Springs, Arkansas**

Childhood Memories of the Great Depression
Copyright © 2009 by Ted Woodworth

For quantity purchases or other information, contact:
email emerald@emeraldink.com
Emerald Ink Publishing, P O Box 2870, Hot Springs, AR 71914

Editor, Ellen Bennett
Back cover poem: Rebecka Woodworth Morse

ISBN # 978-1-885373-29-8

Library of Congress Cataloging in Publication Data:

Woodworth, Ted A.
Childhood memories of the Great Depression Era:
stories as seen through the eyes of a nine-year old boy
in the year 1931 / Ted A. Woodworth.
p. cm. -- (The Black Walnut Farm series)
ISBN 978-1-885373-29-8 (pbk. : alk. paper)
1. Woodworth, Ted A.--Childhood and youth. 2.
Depressions--1929--United States. 3. Poor--United
States--Biography. 4. Boys--United States--Biogra-
phy. I. Title.
CT275.W673A3 2005
973.91'6'092--dc22

2004027015

Emerald Ink Publishing
Printed in the United States of America

CONTENTS

The Parsonage 1

All Catholics are Fat, Rich, and Have a Wooden Leg or How
My Father Taught Me to be Prejudiced 5

Wayne Goes to John Babcock's 10

The Barn at the Parsonage 14

Beatty Hostetler and His Side-car "Motorcycle" 19

Three Trees Short of an Orchard 23

Nina, Forrest, and Bob Aldrich 27

Charles Goes To Work On The Merrill Eaton Farm 31

Let's Have Our Dessert First! 35

LeRoy A. Foster — Lawyer and Poet 39

Staying Overnight With the Shrock's 43

That Reminds Me of the Time 46

How to Quit Smoking—Before You Begin 49

Sheep Shearing Time at the Aaron Marker Farm 53

Rover Takes a Short Vacation 56

The Practical Joker and His Bucking Bronco 60

The Wedding and the Shivaree 64

The Piano Playing Coal Deliveryman 68

The Inventor's Wife 71

The Rigsbys from Kentucky 74

"Pete, The Berry Picker," and His Friend, "Little John" 78

The "Niley" Davis Family 81

Spying on our Neighbors, he Ed Shrock Family 84

I Remember Cecil Christler's Geese 88

The Fruit Cellar 91

I Remember Dan Lobsiger 94

Learning a New Baseball Rule 98

Toddy Bontrager 101

Saylor School.. 105

Go Sit In The First Grade Row, Ted!............................. 109

My First Black Eye—Almost! 112

The County Commissioner...116

George Dintaman, Psychologist and Farmer..................... 121

William Sherman Kerns, Sr. Father of Fifteen 124

The Todd Family Reunion 128

 Mama's Cat, Named Ed, & Other Cats I've Known 132

The Squirting Lapel Flower 136

A Matter of Conscience... 140

Grandmother's Chair 144

Carl Dintaman, Son of George.. 148

How to Show Love to Your Children 152

Fried Chicken With All the Trimmings
at the Merrill Eaton Farm Oh! How I Loved It! 155

A Dinner You'll Never Forget.. 159

Raising a Garden at the Parsonage.................................... 162

The Robbins Family Reunion—1932 166

The "Rube" Foltz Family
& Edna Summey's New Ford V-8 171

Doing it-the Old Fashioned Way 174

The Lost Dime 177

May I Sleep in Your Barn Tonight, Mister?........................ 181

Evicted Again... 185

THE STORY TELLER

Once upon a time long ago,
There was a "Great Depression."
Didn't you know?

Now, to let people know of this period in time,
There came a great storyteller,
And he did just fine.

He told of his family, brothers, sisters and friends,
How he "Grew Up Poor," and the message it sends.

As seen through a child's eyes,
Each story is true.

All people can listen, even relate to his tales.

They'll smile, and laugh,
They might even wail.

Now, you ask with this poem, why bother?

With pride I'll answer,
"The storyteller is my father!"

1

The Parsonage

"You gonna be the preacher, Dad?"

"Don't you go gettin' smart with me, Ted! Just because we're going to be living in the parsonage it doesn't mean I'm going to be the preacher. As a matter of fact, I don't calculate intending to start going to church."

And he didn't. Even though we lived in the parsonage, right next to the Bethel Church for at least a year, I don't recall his going to church once in all that time.

"You and your mother can go to church tomorrow, but I'll just stay here and read the Bible by myself." And that's the way it happened. We went to church and he stayed home reading the Bible.

It was Saturday night and we'd gotten everything moved from the farm that we were going to move. Not everything was arranged or put away, but we were moved.

I didn't like it one bit. All my brothers and sisters were gone and Mom had a job working for the county starting Monday. Then there'd be just Dad and me. I couldn't imagine us getting along together all that well. We hadn't any interests in common and, "Let's face it," I thought, "Dad's an old man. After all, he's 45 already." Seemed old to me.

My eldest sister, Edie, had gone to work for the Paul Dunten family and my sister, Mary, was now the wife of Truman Oesch. That alliance came in handy because he had used his feed truck to move our furniture. Truman worked for his brother, Dan, who owned the Topeka Roller Mills.

Brother Lloyd had been sent to work on the "Abe" Hostetler farm. He didn't mind all that much because their son, Beatty, was his best friend.

1

Charles became a part of the Merril Eaton family. Their farm was less than a mile from the Bethel Church, so he wound up living closer to us than any of my other brothers or sisters. He and I attended the same one room-one teacher eight grades-school. It was named Saylor School after an early settler whose name was William Saylor. It figures. Just like Green School had been named after my great grand-father, whose name was James Green.

And lastly, there was my brother Wayne, closest to me in age. Grandpa Todd had arranged for him to stay with the John Babcocks whose farm adjoined Grandpa's. He was expected to do chores to pay for his board and room.

Nearly everybody in the county was having more than their fair share of problems, just making ends meet. Nobody wanted any extra burdens and that's the only reason I didn't go to live with a strange family. At age nine, I wasn't old enough to carry my own load.

As it turned out, Dad and I got along very well. He spent his time working or looking for work. Sometimes he did neither. Just sat around town talking with other men who were also unemployed and discouraged. They told stories and reminisced and laughed in an effort to bolster each other's morale. And then again, there were times we worked together shearing sheep.

Moving to a new home afforded me an excellent opportunity for exploration, considering I had more than my share of little boy curiosity.

The parsonage had stood vacant since the preacher had been forced to move down the road a ways and take up farming. The members of the congregation were having trouble taking care of their own family needs. For that reason, when the collection plate was passed at the Bethel Church, it generally came back with nothing but small change in it and not much of that.

In exploring the house, I found some things in the basement left by the previous tenants. There were empty fruit jars and even a few with fruit in them. Most looked like they had been canned for at least ten years. Some old pots and pans that should have been thrown out. An old lantern that still worked and some mouse traps. Mostly, just lots of junk. The house was long and had two stories. The kitchen was large, but there was no pantry. One thing it had that we didn't have on the farm, was running water. What a fine luxury! But, it didn't have an inside toilet. My memory says the church members had to use an outside privy as well.

In addition to the kitchen, there was an oversize living room and a bedroom on the ground floor. The upstairs had three bedrooms, as I recall. For some reason, I don't think there were any closets. Just bedrooms.

The house was painted white and there was a red barn. There were a lot of pieces of old harness hanging from the walls. Collars, hames straps, hames tugs, bridles, single trees. You name it, it was there. No matter. We didn't have a horse. Dad kept his Model T in the barn.

We'd been in the house for several days before I heard Dad complaining about there being mice living with us. He'd heard them the night before when he was sitting in the kitchen reading the paper. Said he could hear them "working" in the basement.

After everything had been put away, when we moved in, the basement had quite a lot of our winter food in it. Dad had loaded I don't know how many bags of potatoes into the truck. Dad would have starved to death without his potatoes. Then there were the bags of navy beans. Most everything else was in fruit jars, crocks or lard cans.

Still, Dad didn't want any mice in the house. Afraid they'd get into the potatoes or beans. Nor did he take kindly to having a cat under foot. But, he preferred a cat to the mice.

Besides me, Mom was the one who liked cats. She'd brought a big Tabby cat, named Ed, from the farm. Dad sent me outside to try and lure Ed into the house, hoping he'd take care of the mouse problem. In no time at all I had Ed down in the basement.

There's no telling what happened after I put Ed in the basement but shortly thereafter it sounded like a miniature war had erupted. Ed was yowling and there was glass breaking. What a racket!

Dad grabbed up the kerosene lamp and headed for the basement door. When he opened it Ed almost knocked him down trying to get out of the basement. Dad went on down the stairs. There was broken glass fruit jars all over the floor.

Ed was banished from the house and that's when I remembered seeing the mouse traps in the basement when we first moved in. I showed Dad where they were. Using some pieces of bacon rind for bait, Dad set all three of the traps on the stairway. It was my job to clean up the broken glass next day.

After setting the traps, Dad settled down with his newspaper again. Within five minutes, SNAP! He had one. And as he told it the next morning, the snapping kept on at that rate for over an hour. He'd take the trap and mouse outdoors and throw the mouse to Ed. Then he'd set the trap again and go back to his newspaper.

He caught them all and Ed kept the mouse population in check the rest of the time we lived in "The Parsonage."

2

All Catholics
Are Fat, Rich, and Have a Wooden Leg

or

How My Father Taught Me
to be Prejudiced

In the "olden days" farm children had a very limited number of friends and acquaintances, as a general rule. This can be attributed to the lack of transportation and good roads or just parents that didn't care to or couldn't afford to travel. In my particular case, up until I was nine years old, the only people I knew were either neighbors, schoolmates, or relatives. On our infrequent trips to town, we saw what looked like a throng of people of all ages, sizes and manner of dress. But we didn't actually get to know any of them or anything about them. So that's why I can make the truthful statement, "Until I was nine, the only people I knew were neighbors, schoolmates or relatives."

My schoolmates, and the others I've mentioned, were either Mennonites or Methodists, nigh without exception. Anything else was either unheard of or untalked about.

Dad was known to refer to anybody not speaking English or Dutch as "foreigners." As a matter of fact, he kind of felt everybody to be foreign except those of German or Irish extraction. Whether they intend to or not, parents pass along to their children many unjust and uncalled for prejudices. Young ones normally trust their mother or father implicitly and believe everything their parents tell them. Parents need to be mindful of that trait. Innuendos and half truths become fact to impressionable young children.

Case in point:

One Saturday morning an old stake-bed truck pulled into the driveway of the parsonage. The driver parked under a tree close to the house. I was already out the back door before the truck came to a complete stop. We didn't get much company and I'd never seen this outfit or its driver before.

"Levi the Junk Dealer," it said on the door of his vehicle. As the man stepped out of the truck, he took off his hat. He didn't have much hair and he wasn't as tall as me. I was big for being just barely nine years old. One thing he had plenty of. Nose. It was indeed a big one.

"Is the Parson at home, young feller?" he asked me. I didn't get a chance to answer because Dad had stepped out of the house in time to hear the question. Right off, he took a dislike to the man. Pa didn't want anybody calling him Parson."

"What can we do for you, Mister?" Dad's voice didn't sound as friendly as his words.

"Just wanted to see if you might have some old junk you'd like me to haul away for you." He sounded as though he wanted to do us a favor.

"I just might be able to come up with something I'd be willing to sell you, but give away? NO!" Dad turned to walk back into the house.

"Hold on, Parson!" The man called out.

Quicker'n a wink, Dad wheeled around and all but shouted, "I'm not the Parson and if you know what's good for you, you'll stop calling me that. Be on your way! Empty-handed!"

Levi, that was the name on the door of his truck, wasn't about to give up. I believe he thought Dad was a real challenge. "No! Wait! I meant I wanted to buy from you, and I'm sorry I called you Parson. I didn't know. After all, you do live in the parsonage."

He had a point and Dad knew it. "Well, just living here doesn't make me a "Parson," as you called him. The preacher lives down the road west of here. We're just renting. Now, what is it you're interested in buying?"

"Old iron farming tools, aluminum pots or pans. Maybe you've got a copper wash boiler you don't need. Anything you threw away, I'll take a look at it. If it's something I can use, I'll pay cash for it."

Cash! The magic word! Levi had Dad's undivided attention. "Well now, we just might be able to find something you can use."

It took a while but finally they had assembled together a fair-sized pile of things Dad was willing to sell. There was a three-section spike tooth drag. It was really old and rusty. Then, several old plow parts, a beat up copper wash boiler, and some of the assortment of harness hanging in the barn.

"What do you think it's worth?" Levi asked Dad.

"At least $5.00." Dad answered real quick.

"You must be pulling my leg! It's not worth more than a dollar."

"I might take $4.50 for it," Dad said.

Back and forth they went until Dad finally settled for $2.25. Levi paid him in cash and down the road he went in a cloud of dust.

"Did you see how he 'jewed' us down from $5.00, Ted? Those Jews are all alike. Did you notice his accent? You can be certain he talks Yiddish when he's with his family. We can sure use the $2.25, but he'll make money on it. It's a well known fact that Jews can make money on what poor people throw away."

I was glad he had the money, too, because it meant we'd eat better at least for a few days. Dad hadn't had any work for a while.

The sad part of it was I'd picked up another prejudice in that short encounter.

Another time, in the middle of the morning, a salesman stopped by. We didn't want any of whatever it was he was selling. After he drove away in his shiny black Model "A" Ford, Dad had some observations to make about him. "Did you notice his black eyes?" We all had blue eyes. "And that coal black hair all slicked back on his head? Looked like he had grease on it. He probably thought only women would be at home. He was a woman chaser! They all are!"

"Who you talking about, Dad? Who was he?"

"For one thing, he was a salesman. And he was a Wop! They're all a bunch of Gigolos. Like as not he was a Catholic to boot."

Mom had to explain to me later what he had meant, but Dad had succeeded in planting some more prejudice. Salesmen, Italians, and Catholics. No good. View them with suspicion.

Fortunately, as I grew older, I was able to form my own opinions and many of them were poles apart from my father's. But, let me tell you about the first time I met a Catholic and the conclusions I drew from the meeting.

His name was John and he was an "inmate" (for lack of a better word) at the County Farm, otherwise known as the "Poor Farm." On several of my visits to see my mother, the "hired girl." I would wander through the long, plain, building behind the big main house. It was where most of the men lived. This one man showed an interest in me and I in him. He told me stories of his adventures as a young man and I hung on his every word. I liked him partly because he treated me like a real person. He talked to me. John was a big man. A very big man! He always seemed to be sitting with one leg resting on a chair or a bench. You see, he had a wooden leg. One day I asked him about the cross he wore on a chain around his neck. That's when he told me he was a Catholic. I was surprised! John wasn't what I had expected a Catholic to be like. I don't actually know just what I did expect, but not John. On another visit, he asked me how much spending money my father gave me and I told him, none. "Haven't you ever had any money?" John sounded as though he didn't believe me. When I told him, no, he said, "We're going to change that right now." With that, he took out his coin purse, unsnapped it, and carefully selected a shiny Indian head nickel. When he handed it to me I just

held it in the palm of my hand and looked at it. I'd never had one before. Talk about making an impression on someone!

Right then was when I decided, *All Catholics are fat, and rich, and have a wooden leg.* Dad would have been proud of me. Even though only nine years old, I had made a determination about a group of people that I knew absolutely nothing about.

3

Wayne Goes to John Babcock's

It was a dark day in my brother Wayne's life. He was going to be separated from his family for the first time ever. Never before, even for one night had he been away from home.

"Don't make me go, Papa. Let me stay with you and Ted. You'll see. I'll be a lot of help. I'll take care of you and this winter I can turn the crank while you tag sheep." Wayne didn't want to go.

"Ted can do the housework while your Mother's gone. He's nine and big enough to turn the crank too, so he can just as well furnish all the help I need with the sheep shearing." Dad didn't want to separate the family either, but it seemed like the only way.

"But, Papa, Ted doesn't know how to use the wool board to tie the fleeces into bundles. I can do that. After all, I'm already twelve years old and big for my age. Please, Papa! I promise to be good and I won't cause you any trouble." His pleadings were lost on Dad because it had already been decided.

"You can come home on weekends, sometimes, like your mother will be doing. You'll be right next door to your Grandpa and Grandma Todd. You can go see them real regular. Won't that be nice?" It was as hard on Dad as it was on Wayne.

"Why can't I just go and stay with Grandpa and Grandma? They're family and it wouldn't be so much of a change."

"Well, to begin with, they must not hanker for the idea because it was your Grandfather who arranged for you to stay with the Babcocks. Your Grandma is practically an invalid since she got both her legs broken in that wreck. She has to have somebody take care of her let alone her having to look after you when Joe is away painting." Grandpa was a painter in addition to being a farmer.

"But, Dad . . ." Wayne was still protesting.

"All right! All right!" Dad was getting exasperated. To put it mildly, he was running out of patience. "I've told you. I don't need you! The reason he needs somebody is that his only son, Clark, got married this past June, to Irene Nelson, and they've gone to live in Sturgis. Clark is 23 and wanted to get out on his own. So you see? John needs some help and you're going to be it."

"I'll go, but I'd still feel better about it if they were 'family.'" Wayne was ready to give in. His protestations had been in vain. He felt unwanted and abandoned.

Dad had one final, convincing, argument and he felt certain it would put Wayne's mind at ease. "What if I told you the Babcock's actually are 'family'?"

This caused Wayne's ears to prick up. He'd never heard we were related to the Babcocks.

"Now pay attention," Dad said, "because I'm only going to tell it once."

"Back in 1836, a man by the name of John Y. Clark bought a section of good farm land out east and a little south of LaGrange. A section is a mile square or 640 acres. He and his wife raised a family there including two sons named William and Abraham.

"On a slight hill, on this section, John Clark built a house that was later occupied by William and his wife, Mary. William died. Their daughter, Grace, married John Babcock and they and her mother, Mary, live on the farm now.

"The house, where your grandparents live, was built by Abraham Clark and he later sold it to your Grandpa, Joe Todd."

"What's that got to do with us? How does that make them 'family'?" Wayne was trying hard to follow along.

"I'm coming to it! I'm coming to it!

"Your Grandfather was brought up in that same area and his father's name was, 'Clark' Todd. Don't you see? It's got to be more than a coincidence. They're 'family'!" Dad finished with a big smile and with what he hoped was a convincing look on his face.

Wayne wasn't convinced. "I told you I'd go, so, let's go."

In short order, they were headed for the John Babcock farm in Dad's old Model T Ford.

As it turned out, Wayne got along just fine with John and Grace Babcock. But Grace's mother, Mary, was his favorite. He was impressed by how well she got around on crutches. You see, she only had one leg.

Wayne had learned at home how to milk a cow, so he helped with the milking as well as with other chores. He liked feeding the horses their hay and didn't mind feeding the sheep and hogs. The main reason he was partial to the horses was because they'd let him sit on their backs.

Sometimes, when Wayne would get home from school, John would let him ride one of the horses to go after the milk cows. Wayne didn't have any problem because he'd been riding our horse, Barney, for several years.

Wayne found out real fast that he wasn't going to have much chance to be bored or lonesome. In addition to going to school, he was allowed to cut through the orchard to go see Grandpa and Grandma Todd, after his chores were done. Oftentimes, he'd stay for supper.

There was another attraction nearby. Across the road from Babcock's lived the Shelley family. Vern and Margaret Shelley had three children. There were two boys, named Phillip and Lloyd, and a girl, named Dorothy. They were all somewhere near Wayne's age, although Phil was closer to my age. He and I became good friends in later years. I remember he was a near genius in mathematics.

The school was another new challenge. Wayne had always gone to Green School and now he would be entering the sixth grade at Huff Corners. His teacher was Donald Beaty. Wayne felt like he knew Mr. Beaty having seen him a time or two at the "pickle factory" in LaGrange. Vern Beaty, Donald Beaty's dad, ran the "pickle factory" where our dad always sold the cucumbers we raised on the farm. We had a contract with Vern Beaty.

Our cousin, Keith Todd, was in Wayne's class at Huff Corners School. That helped immeasurably. It also made a good arrangement for Wayne to go home with Keith once in a while. That way he got to spend some time with cousins, Jack and Robert, as well as with Uncle Lewis and Aunt Marie.

More than once, Uncle Henry and Aunt Eva Todd would come, with their children, to visit Grandma and Grandpa. It was always on a weekend, so Wayne would get to spend time with cousins, Leora, Ruth, Warren and Janette. Warren was only a year younger than Wayne and they had lots of fun playing together.

Now that I think of it, Warren and Jack and I had an outstanding comradely feeling toward each other. But, that's another story.

Those were difficult days, indeed. The only solution was to "grin and bear it" and that's what we did.

4

The Barn at the Parsonage

Exploration time again!

School was due to start first week in September and I had plenty of leisure time to do as I pleased. I just may have been a little bit more adventurous than most boys, so I pretty much kept on the move all the time. There were only about two or three acres to explore and the back half of it was a really big garden space. I knew for sure Dad would ask one of the neighbors to plow it up for him next spring — early. He'd want to be the first one planting early red potatoes. He generally was. Dad was definitely a potato lover.

The big garden lot was completely surrounded by a wire fence. Most of the back part of it had a green vine, called bitter-sweet, growing on it. The vines were beautiful because, through the dark green leaves, you could see they were just loaded with the bright orange berries that would stay on the vines long after the leaves had fallen off.

My mother used to cut bunches of the berries and dry them. They'd stay on the branches all winter long. Mom was always trying to add color to wherever she was.

Back along the fence I found places in the grass where it was pretty obvious cotton tail rabbits had made their nests. When wild grass is left to grow, it often seems to climb up a couple of feet on the fence. It's easy for a rabbit to find protection right in or near the fence. They're really "snug as a bug in a rug" when it snows and covers up all the grass and their nest.

On the east side of the garden there were wild raspberry bushes growing in the fence row. I just knew I'd be back when the berries would start to ripen in the spring.

Immediately behind the church were several big shade trees. I never thought of myself as being a bird watcher, but I spent a lot of time lying on the grass watching the birds in the trees. And then there was watching the clouds and conjuring up all kinds of explanations for the different shapes that clouds form. There were always lots of beautiful mountains. There would be camels and whales, not to mention old men with beards. You name it and a young boy can imagine it.

Living on a much more heavily traveled road had some advantages. I used to sit in the front yard and watch the cars go by. For one thing, I didn't know there were so many kinds of automobiles. Most of them I wasn't able to identify because I had mostly seen only Ford Model T's and Model A's.

There was one distinct disadvantage to all the traffic. The road was gravel and the cars raised lots of dust. The house wasn't insulated all that well, so that meant the floors, furniture, and everything else, always seemed to be covered with dust. Many times I had been in the Bethel Church building, but exploring it from belfry to basement, while it was empty, was a new experience. It was always unlocked, so I could come and go as I pleased.

The barn was built much differently than the one had been on our farm or the one on the Black Walnut Farm. Without the aid of a long ladder, it would have been next to impossible to have climbed onto the roof of either of those two barns. Not so—the one at the parsonage. One side, as I recall, had a granary running nearly the full length of the barn. There were stalls on the back side. The roof on the long side, opposite the granary, came nearly to the ground.

My brothers used to go hand over hand along the hay track inside the barn, but I'm just certain none of them ever climbed to the ridge peak of a barn on the outside. It was steep and probably dangerous, but I did it many times.

What a magnificent view! And, as long as I just peeked over the top, nobody could see me. What a splendid opportunity to spy on our new neighbors! Actually, we were the new neighbors. They had been there well before we came. But, you know what I mean.

Across the road, and west a bit, I could see Cecil Christler's farm and buildings. Closer to me was a smaller house where I think his father lived. I could see it plainly. In the other direction the trees behind the church obscured my view somewhat, but my imagination did the rest. It sounded like rain as the wind blew gently through the cottonwood trees. Surely, in winter, I would have a perfect view in that direction.

Across from the church or nearly so-was the cemetery. It had been used, as a graveyard, for many years. Some of the grave markers were dated more than 50 years before. It was a spooky place to visit, but I did visit it anyway.

There was a small field between us and our closest neighbors, who lived on the farm west of us. They were Ed and Fannie Shrock. Their daughter, Alma, was older than me. Paul was my same age and Silas, Martha, Homer Peter, and Phyllis, were younger. We eventually became very close friends and it's a good thing for we surely did spend a lot of time together. More time, beyond a doubt, than their parents would have liked.

Ed Shrock was known to have delivered the Sunday sermon at the Shore Mennonite Church from time to time. This put him in a position where he felt his children needed to be good examples to the other young ones in the congregation.

I probably shouldn't have said that. In looking back, it's likely he just wanted his children to follow Bible principle. Included would have been, obeying your parents, and avoiding bad associations.

After school, each night I walked home with the Shrock children. We discussed many different topics, some related to school and some not. There's little doubt we had an influence on each other. For instance, I was impressed with the fact they hurried, rather than dawdled, on the way home from school. As they put it, "There's chores that need doing.

Somehow, there seems often to be an exception to any rule.

One afternoon, just shortly after we started the fall school term, the subject of "geese" came up. Paul said, "Cecil Christler has a flock of geese. They lay just about the biggest eggs you've ever seen. Not only that, he's got several ganders in the bunch. They're real mean."

"Geese are nothing but big ducks and I've seen them, but what's a 'gander?" I couldn't remember ever having seen one.

Paul said to Alma, "Let's take Ted down to the Christler's and show him. It's only a little ways and we can hurry back."

Alma didn't really think it was such a good idea, but she agreed.

The whole front yard was fenced so the geese couldn't get out on the road, but there they were, just slowly walking along, eating.

Suddenly, three big birds ran toward us making a loud hissing sound! Their wings were outstretched, it looked like six feet. I just knew they were going to fly. We ran, not knowing whether or not they could come right over or even through the fence. They didn't, but we never stopped running until we were back at the Shrock farm house.

I don't know. Maybe I was bad associations. Paul and Alma both got spanked and told not to go down to the Christler's again.

1923 FORD, Model T, Fordor Sedan

5

Beatty Hostetler
and
His Side-car "Motorcycle"

Every adult has memories of one or more people who exercised a tremendous influence over them during their formative years. I had several. One of them was John Beatty Hostetler. My brother, Lloyd, always called him Beatty. That was his Mother's maiden name—I think. Young boys tend to emulate their older brothers and I was no exception, so, I called him Beatty also.

During the year we lived in the parsonage of the Bethel Church, Lloyd used to come home on weekends especially on those when Mom was home from her job at the County Hospital. His visits were always a joyous occasion to me, especially when he brought one of his friends. I shouldn't say, "He brought one of his friends" because they brought him. Lloyd didn't have a car at the time.

No doubt about it, Beatty Hostetler was Lloyd's best friend. When they came to the parsonage it was on one of Beatty's motorcycles. Over a period of time, he owned six or seven different ones.

Beatty often used to buy a second hand Harley Davidson or an Indian motorcycle that was in need of repair. After fixing whatever was wrong, using a major application of elbow grease, cleaning, waxing and polishing, it would begin to look like new. Then, Beatty would either sell it outright or "trade up to get a better one.

There were two Indian's and three or four Harley Davidsons. When he got through working on one, it looked like new. Because of his hard work, he made out reasonably well financially. But then whatever Beatty did, he always gave it his "best shot" as they say now. I think his motto was, "If it's worth doing, it's worth doing right." And too, my memory says he always finished what he started.

Beatty and his motorcycles were always very "spit and polished." He always looked like he had just stepped out of a band box, as the feller says. The motorcycle was always polished to a high gloss.

As a general rule, Beatty wore black clothes. Black shiny boots, black breeches, black shirt, black leather jacket, black leather cap with goggles, and a black belt that must have been more than six inches wide. It was tightened in such a way that it forced him to hold his back very straight and erect. I thought he looked very grand. Just about the whole outfit was leather. It afforded excellent protection if he lost control and took a spill.

I almost forgot! He also wore black leather gloves.

Once, Beatty had a really heavy Harley Davidson parked in the grass in our back yard. The kick stand was down but, as it slowly sank into the grass, the motorcycle fell over onto its side.

Now, at this time, Beatty didn't weigh 125 pounds soaking wet and with his leather boots, belt and jacket on. There was some question as to whether or not he could get it back on its wheels by himself. But, with a lot of effort and determination, he did. Like the feller says, "The only thing better than a good big man is a good little man.

During some of the time Beatty was "into" motorcycles, he'd let Lloyd ride one of his bikes and he'd ride another. So, occasionally they'd show up with two motorcycles and, when that happened, I always got to ride on the back with one of them. Sometimes they'd both take me for a ride. I always considered it to be an outstanding climax to the week no matter what had taken place earlier.

While we lived in the parsonage, I attended Saylor School, and was in the fourth grade. Lloyd was a Junior at Shipshewana High School and Beatty was in the same grade.

Lloyd got along well in school, according to Beatty, and he got good grades. The only problem area was his deportment. He was prone to "sound off" when the mood struck him. You know-let out an exuberant shout when quiet was reigning. He once explained to a teacher, after a loud outburst, "I couldn't help myself. It was like spontaneous combustion. I had to let it out ere I'd explode."

On another occasion, a teacher was loudly berating him for having disrupted the class. After delivering her harangue, the teacher said, "No more of it! Do I make myself clear?"

Lloyd's immediate response was, "Your vociferous expostulations are positively too copious for my diminutive comprehension."

The class roared with laughter and the teacher threw up her hands in despair. "I give up!" She said, as she stormed out of the classroom and slammed the door. Lloyd liked to use big words.

Mom got to come home every other Saturday and Sunday. On one of those Sundays, Beatty and Lloyd came to visit riding a vehicle I'd never seen before. It was a motorcycle with a side-car. Beatty was astride the bike and Lloyd was riding in the side car.

When they had parked this "contraption," Dad called it, I just walked around it, "gawking." The motorcycle itself was a big one. I knew it wasn't a Harley Davidson nor was it an Indian. Then I saw the name on the side of the gas tank. It was a "Henderson." I'd never seen one before.

Mom looked it over too, and allowed as how it probably wasn't safe. Me? I couldn't wait to be invited to ride in it.

The road in front of the parsonage was gravel, as were all the country roads. They weren't very wide. True, they were wide enough to pass another car but, normally, you drove in the middle of the road. And, since it was a gravel road, cars would make the dust really fly.

Then it happened! Beatty said, "You want to go for a ride, Ted?"

"I sure do!" And in a flash, I was seated in the side car. In those days, Motorcycles didn't have automatic starters. The rider first had to flip out the step part of the foot starter. After carefully balancing the motorcycle, he'd put his foot on the starter then suddenly bring all his weight to bear on the pedal. It's hard to describe the motion, but it was something like that.

When the motorcycle started, the motor had an almost deafening roar. Beatty pushed down on the clutch and shifted into low gear. Slowly letting out the clutch pedal, we took off in a cloud of dust. There were three different gears so he had to change gears as we picked up speed.

We drove to the crossroads by the Saylor School and turned around to head back toward the house. It was just an even mile. Dad had said that Beatty had a heavy foot and now I knew what he meant. It seemed as though we were nearly flying as we passed the Olmstead Farm. Right at that point, Beatty tilted the Henderson toward him until the side car lifted clean off the road.

And, that's the position we were in when we passed the parsonage. Mom, Dad, and Lloyd were in front of the house, watching. Mom had her hand over her mouth, trying vainly to stifle a scream. "I was scared stiff!" she said later.

I thought it was great fun and wasn't at all afraid. Why should I be afraid? After all, Beatty wasn't afraid. And that's the way it was. Beatty Hostetler was one of my role models when I was growing up.

6

Three Trees Short of an Orchard

Jacob Yoder and I stood in the front yard of his new home on a back corner of The Black Walnut Farm. It's not exactly on a hill but we were able to see quite a distance in all four directions. Jacob's grown children lived in four of the houses within our sight.

"Did you know that my great-grandfather, James Green, once owned all the farmland we are able to see from here-and then some?" I thought I was probably telling Jacob something that he didn't already know. But, not so. His answer was, "Yes, I knew that, Ted. James Green owned an impressive chunk of this area." Jacob and his family own most of it now.

As we talked, we reminisced about times gone by. All of his children and many of his grandchildren had attended Green School, so the memory of James Green would always be with him. We talked about the farm across the road, where he had lived for over forty years, and the adjoining one where I had been born. In 1930 through 1933 Ed Shrock and his family had lived on the farm behind Jacob's.

Also, I had a visit with Paul Shrock, Ed's son, whom I hadn't seen since 1932 when we were both in fourth grade at Saylor School. But, that'll have to wait until another time.

Jacob and his neighbors are members of The Old Order Amish Church. When I drove into his front yard, he was busy swinging a hammer. "Building calf houses," he said.

After finishing our "Hellos" and "How have you beens?" I asked, "Isn't it about time you retired, Jacob?"

He laughed at the word "retired." "I turned the farms over to my boys and now I have time to catch up on the things I never seemed to have time for. Retire? Not me!

23

"However, there is one thing I don't do any more of. Plowing. I had what's known as a 'farm accident' and, when it happened, I thought of you, Ted."

"Really? Just why would an accident cause you to think of me?" I was anxious to find out.

"Well, you're always telling stories about how your dad and brothers picked stones off these fields. You said your father complained that for every 25 bushels of corn he raised per acre, he'd also get 60 bushels of stones."

That was true. The only difference was I called them rocks and Jacob called them stones. He must be right. I've never heard of a "rock boat" but I sure know what a "stone boat" is for.

Jacob went on, "The boys have been complaining for years that the fields on the old farm weren't laid out properly. It never came out even, when they plowed. I knew that and I knew what the problem was. The lane to the woods wasn't laid out right. It was straight but it wasn't straight with the fields. Your Great-Grandpa Green must have laid it out." And then he laughed. But he was probably right.

"Well, we fixed it. Moved the fences over. The lane was off about 24 feet from one end to the other which was almost exactly the width of the lane. "Anyway, I volunteered to plow this long triangular strip, which had been the lane. Hadn't been plowed in years. You know what? I nearly killed myself. I was driving a team of four horses pulling a single bottom plow. It didn't take long for me to discover that the full length of the lane must have once been used as a stone pile. Just beneath the sod there were about a jillion stones.

"The horses hadn't been worked for a while and were acting kind of feisty. They were rarin' to go. In short order, the plow hit a big stone so hard that, before I could I could catch myself, I was thrown off the plow with such force that I landed at least ten feet away and against a fence post.

"Were you hurt?" I wanted to know.

"Yes, I was hurt! As a matter of fact I was laid up for several days. That was the end of my plowing. I may not be retired from working but I'm definitely retired from plowing."

"Can't say I blame you. But, just exactly how did your plowing accident remind you of me? You still haven't told me." I wasn't going to let him get by without a clear explanation.

Jacob took out his well worn red bandanna and wiped his brow. After he'd put it away he kind of stroked his gray beard. With a mischievous grin he said, "Why Ted, I never see a pile of stones and don't think of you. And, the other way around. I never see you that I don't think of stones. It's pretty obvious your ancestors picked a lot of stones off these fields and I'd guess it'll never end.

"Let me explain that. If we have a mild winter, there's hardly any stones at plowing time in the spring. But, let us have a bitter, cold, long winter and the earth pushes up a fresh batch to be picked. There's no end to it. I know you're probably in a hurry to get some place or another, but let me tell you a story before you go." Jacob has a keen talent for one liners or whole stories.

"Never let it be said that I don't have time for a good story. Let's have it."

This is a story about a man who owned a farm very much like the ones we've been talking about. Lots and lots of stones. Several times each year he'd hitch up his team to a stone boat and then spend the whole day picking up stones. He put them all on a pile alongside the woods. But, it was a losing battle.

Finally, this man despaired and decided to give up farming. He offered his place up for sale. Well, everybody in the neighborhood knew about his "rock" farm. None wanted to buy it.

So, the man advertised his farm for sale through a newspaper in the adjoining state.

"Farm for sale. Rich, fertile, productive soil. Priced to sell," the ad read.

Sure enough, in no time at all, here came an out of state car pulling into his driveway.

"Like to have a look at your farm," the man said.

"I'll take you on a tour." The farmer was very obliging. They hadn't gotten half away across the first field when the prospective buyer remarked, "Seems to be an abundance of stones."

"Yes, and aren't you fortunate?"

"In what way?" the man wanted to know.

"Let me pry up one of these stones and I'll show you." With that, he pried up a kind of flat stone about 12 inches across.

"You see how damp it is under the stone? That's why this farm is so fertile and productive. The stones hold the moisture!"

"Well, I do declare!" the man said.

"Just as they were about to return to the house the man spotted the big pile of stones alongside the woods."

"If the stones hold the moisture, as you say, why is that big pile over there by the woods?"

By this time the farmer was sure this out of stater was about three trees short of an orchard and would believe anything, so he answered, "When you buy the farm that'll just be some more of your good fortune! Those stones haven't been spread yet!"

Like I said, "Jacob Yoder has a good sense of humor."

I enjoy talking to him.

7

Nina, Forrest, and Bob Aldrich

Nina was one of Mom's best friends, especially in the later years. Dad thought of her as "Bert" Walters' daughter first and Forrest Aldrich's wife second. Mr. Walters was definitely not one of Dad's favorite people because he was head man at the bank when it went broke. "The Bank" being the one in which Grandpa had lost a bunch of money.

My memory of Nina Aldrich is that she was one of the twelve best cooks in the county. My view might have been slanted due to the circumstances and the time, I'll have to admit.

The first time I remember enjoying Nina's cooking was during the spring of the year Dad and I lived alone at the parsonage. It would be truthful to acknowledge that I didn't turn up my nose at anybody's cooking. A full meal was not something I got with any regularity. "Catch as catch can" would be the appropriate expression. The circumstances were far from ideal. Dad came home early the day before we were scheduled to shear sheep on the Forrest Aldrich farm.

"You'd better get a good night's sleep, Ted. You're going to have to miss school tomorrow and help me shear Forrest Aldrich's sheep. It may take us two days because he has a big flock and then there's Charlie to think about." Dad was kind of smiling when he mentioned Charlie.

"Charlie? What about him?" I was real curious and I didn't have any idea who or what he was talking about. "Charlie's an old hermit that lives by himself in a little house on the Aldrich farm. I always give him a haircut, in the spring, when I shear Forrest's sheep. It's the only haircut he gets all year." Dad acted like he was looking forward to it and I'd have to admit the prospect of his cutting a man's hair with sheep shears sounded interesting. He'd threatened to do that to me a time or two.

The next morning, Dad was up early and rarin' to go. We didn't have any milk so I wound up leaving home without eating breakfast. Again. "You can hold out 'til noon so there's no need to mention not having had breakfast. Understood?"

I understood.

"Nina's a good cook and she'll fix a good dinner. Like as not we'll get to enjoy one of her berry pies. Last year it was raspberry, as I recall. Sure wish she'd bake a gooseberry pie, but I don't think they have any bushes."

Dad was sounding as though it was going to be difficult for him to hold out 'til dinner time.

Dad loaded the sheep shearing machine and the wool box into the back seat of the Model T and we headed east. There wasn't a soul to be seen at the school. Nobody had gotten there yet. Another three miles and we turned back east again onto Road 20. After just a few yards, Dad pulled the car onto the shoulder of the road.

"Look over there, Ted." He was pointing at a big black area of the pavement. Alongside the road, in the ditch and out into the field, there was fresh green grass coming up through blackened stubble. Even the fence posts had been burned and, in some cases, new posts were evident.

"What in the world caused that?" It kind of scared me just to look at it.

"That's where two big semi truck and trailer rigs hit head on late last summer. One was loaded with new bicycles and the other with some kind of industrial machinery. Remember? It was at night and we could see the bright red glow of the fire all the way to the farm."

Then I remembered because we had driven over to see it the next day. The wreckage had still been smoldering and the fire truck was still there. It had looked like two big truck skeletons. Everything had burned that could, even the tires, but I hadn't gotten a good look at what it had done to the road. It must have really burned hot.

"Why did they crash, Dad? Was the road too narrow?"

"For a fact the road is narrow for semis. But, in this case, one of the drivers evidently went to sleep and ended up in the wrong lane."

We drove on to the Aldrich farm a short distance further down the road and on the right side. It was a nice looking farm kind of on the side of a hill. Bob Aldrich was on his way out of the house heading for school. Bob had his own car and my memory says, some short time later, he had a serious accident in which he lost his life.

Forrest had finished his chores already and even had the sheep penned up inside the barn. Dad carried the shearing machine and I carried the wool box into the barn.

All Dad needed was a level dry space on which to work, be it a cement or a dirt floor. It was awfully hard on his knees because one or the other was always on the ground. Forrest insisted on trying to make it easier on Dad.

He put down several forkfuls of straw and then spread a tarp over the top of it. Dad walked over the whole thing several times, to squash it down flatter, then allowed as how he was ready to start to work.

Forrest left to go up to the house for breakfast.

"Well, lookey here, Ted! Shropshires!" Dad hadn't remembered what breed of sheep we were about to shear. He was happy. I was glad. I was always glad to see him happy. It didn't happen that often.

"This'll be easy, huh, Dad?"

"There's no such thing as its being easy to shear any kind of sheep, but this sure beats shearing wrinkly necked Merinos."

Shropshire sheep originated in England and were raised more for their meat than for their wool.

We had sheared two of the fat, smooth skinned, black faced, ewes and had tied up their fleeces in the wool box when Mr. Aldrich came back from breakfast. I was turning the crank and Dad had started to shear when Forrest said "Ted, did you have breakfast before you came here?"

Dad turned and gave me "a look." I kept on turning the crank and didn't answer.

Forrest turned to Dad, "Cecil, Nina made a big pan of hot cocoa and Bob hardly touched it. I'll turn the crank so Ted can go get some of that cocoa. What say?"

"Well," Dad kind of grumbled. "I guess it'd be all right."

I stopped turning and stood back. Forrest put his left foot on the short tripod, as I had done, took hold of the wooden support handle with his left hand and started turning the crank with his right.

"Bring Cecil a cup of coffee when you come back, Ted," he called as I hurried out of the barn and ran up to the house.

Just as I touched the door knob, Nina called out, "Come on in, Ted," and in the same breath, "Wash your hands there in the sink. You can drink some cocoa while I fix you some scrambled eggs and bacon. I must have two helpings of fresh fried potatoes left and plenty of toast. How does that sound?"

I'd never heard words that sounded better and I told her so. I nearly gorged myself, the breakfast was so good.

When I carried a big cup of coffee out to dad, Forrest was glad to see me. Turning the crank wasn't such hard work but it was pretty monotonous.

At dinner, Nina outdid herself. I remember beef and noodles as well as several different cooked vegetables. And, absolutely scrumptious cherry pie. Dad had guessed wrong but it was delicious.

The sheep were so easy to shear that we finished in the middle of the afternoon. Forrest had been watching our progress and, as we were finishing the last one, here he came with Charlie. I can't remember having seen a man with such long hair. He had a white towel with him which he put over his shoulders and under his hair, that hung clear down his back.

Charlie sat on a three legged milk stool. Dad had to lean over but, as I turned the crank, the clippers did the job. It only took a few strokes and Charlie was as bald as an eagle.

I remember thinking, "I wish I could have had a 'before' and an 'after' picture."

Yes, life was hard during the depression, but everybody has some pleasant memories.

8

Charles Goes To Work
On The Merrill Eaton Farm

Late in the summer of 1931, Charles was informed that he was to go live with the Merrill Eaton family. Only Dad and I lived full time in the parsonage of the Bethel Church. The rest of the family had been dispersed thither and yon to, more or less, fend for themselves. Except for Edie and Mom, their pay was board, room, and clothing. None of them liked the idea, especially at first. Dad kept trying to encourage us by saying, "We'll all be back together as a family real soon." But, we never were. Never again.

Merrill and Vera Eaton lived on a farm next to the Saylor School, so Charles enrolled in the seventh grade and continued there until he finished the eighth grade. One thing for sure, he had a number of new experiences at Saylor School, one of which was his first time to fall in love. Well -maybe it wasn't love, but more like -in like. You know what I mean. Whichever it was, it was his first time. Her name was June.

Except for having spent a month at Uncle Charlie Miller's, Charles had never been away from home even overnight. It wouldn't have been so bad if he could have been more certain that it wasn't going to be a permanent arrangement.

Since the Eatons and our family went to Church together we at least weren't strangers. Far from it, as a matter of fact. My folks had been knowing both Merrill and Vera for a good many years. Vera's Dad was "Mac" Dunafin and he still owned the farm where Wellington Bradley lived, just a stones throw from the farm where Charles and I had been born. Vera had grown up there. Charles was thirteen at the time and should have been in the eighth grade. Two broken arms kept him from starting the first grade when he should have. No question about it, he was an active boy.

The Eatons had a son, Robert, who was in the second grade. I used to walk with Robert and Charles as far as their house after school. I had another mile to walk to the parsonage. The Shrock children walked the rest of the way with me, since they lived one farm beyond the parsonage. It was lonesome for me because many times Dad wasn't there yet when I got home from school.

Charles and Robert had to hurry and get home so they could start doing chores. Before they left for school in the morning they had to do chores, as well. It would have seemed Charles wouldn't have had time to get homesick, but he did anyway. Working doesn't keep a person from thinking. On at least one occasion, Charles used the Eaton's phone to call our sister Edie at her work. She was employed in the household of Paul Dunten. Charles got so homesick he was in tears. Edie told him to ask Merrill if he couldn't spend the weekend with Dad and me. That did the trick and that's what he did.

Vera and Merrill thought a lot of Charles, partly because he was a good worker. He was very shy but both of the Eatons were friendly and outgoing. Robert liked Charles too, so it wasn't long before he was like part of the family.

At the Bethel Church, Merrill Eaton was music director. He had a deep voice and sang bass. One of his favorite songs was "On Christ The Solid Rock I Stand." Charles said he thought some of the worshipers came to Church just to hear Merrill sing and direct the congregation in singing. He was one of the Sunday School teachers, too.

Supper time was a real treat for Charles. Vera was a very good cook and it pleased her that Charles liked her cooking. In the spring, they had a strawberry patch that was new to him since we never had them on our farm. Not far away were some neighbors, I think their name was Latta, who had a huckleberry marsh. To Charles' way of thinking, nothing in the whole world tasted better than Vera's huckleberry pie.

Springtime was plowing time and Dad had taught Charles well. He plowed a truly straight furrow. It helped that Merrill had better farming tools than Dad. The fields were more level and square. Virtually no rocks! Charles could barely imagine a farm without lots of rocks of all sizes. It seemed, sometimes, like our farm had more rocks than it had soil. Some weren't rocks but more like boulders. Dad used to say he wished we could harvest as much wheat as we did rocks.

During the last few years we lived on the farm, we didn't have more than one milk cow at a time but Charles definitely knew how to milk cows. Didn't mind a bit. Merrill's had several cows and sold cream.

As did most farmers, he raised some hogs. After the cream had been separated from the milk, the skimmed milk was fed to the hogs. It took the place of "supplement" usually bought from the elevator or feed store. Corn and skimmed milk was mostly all the hogs ate. Well-not all. There was always a five gallon bucket beside the kitchen range. Into it was dumped potato peelings, actually any vegetable peelings, potato water from boiled potatoes, dish water, anything at all left over from cooking. The hogs loved it! We called it slop.

Slop, indeed! Modern dieticians would say the farmers fed the hogs the most nutritional and healthful part of the vegetables and milk. Maybe not the dishwater, but it was good for them, too. After all, there would have been soap in the dishwater. There was lye in the soap used then. Most worming medications for hogs had lye in it. No wonder they got fat on what was thrown away. It was good for them.

Cranking the DeLaval separator was one chore Charles looked forward to. After the discs and all had been put together, the bowl filled with milk, and the buckets in place to catch the cream in one and the skim milk in the other, it was time to start turning the crank. I never knew exactly how a separator worked but I'm nearly certain it had something to do with centrifugal force. However it worked, Charles enjoyed turning the crank faster and faster until a sort of bell sounded indicating the mechanisms were moving fast enough to separate the cream from the milk. At that time he'd turn the little spigot on that let the whole milk start running out of the bowl into the separator. Then, the handle was easy to turn.

This was the part Charles liked best. He now started retrieving cookies out of his pants pockets and eating them. You see, he'd help himself from the cookie jar when he was getting the clean separator parts from where Vera kept them in the pantry. He did it all the time he worked there and thought he was getting away with something. It wasn't until years later Vera told him she knew about it all the time. How? Every time she'd wash his overalls she'd have to shake the cookie crumbs out of his pants pockets.

It just goes to show, you can't hide anything from the one who does your laundry.

The Merrill Eaton Family
Eva and Merrill
with Robert, Glendon and Daryl

9

Let's Have Our Dessert First!

"There's more than one way to skin a cat."
"There's two sides to every coin."
"There's two sides to every story."
The "old saying" I'm going to pursue at this time is,
"There's more than one way to tell a story."

A couple of years ago I had the privilege of making several announcements to an assembled group of some 200 persons. As I read over the various announcements beforehand, I became aware of one which I felt was of greater interest to the congregation than the others were. My first inclination was to save it to last. All of the announcements were of interest and important, but this one would be the icing on the cake. Then, ham that I am, I decided to tell a story.

Here's the story I told:

When I was a lad of nine, I walked from the house where we lived to the handsome farm of my Uncle Austin and Aunt Alice Merriman. It was close to five miles but I didn't mind. Not only was their farm a model for the community but the house and the outbuildings were painted and well taken care of.

I was impressed by the imposing four story brick house. It was surely a big one, with many rooms. And, of all the luxuries a small boy could dream about, the house had an elevator! It was the first I'd ever seen—let alone ridden in.

It was kind of late in the afternoon when I got there. Uncle Austin and the hired man, as well as "Little John," had just finished milking the cows. Uncle Austin invited me to stay for supper, but I declined. "I'm going to have to head for home in a little bit. It's a long walk and I don't want to be walking in the dark."

"Don't worry about it," Uncle Austin said. "I'll drive you home after supper. And besides, I'm just sure I saw the cook baking some big lemon meringue pies."

That was an offer I couldn't refuse. Pie was one of my favorite foods. Mother was there also, and naturally she made sure I washed my face and hands, as well as comb my hair, before I came to the table.

It was a big table with plenty of room. Uncle Austin sat at the head of the table and I at the foot. Aunt Alice was on my right and Mom was at my left. Next to Mom was the hired girl whose name was Ruth Grimm. She was up and down, waiting on the rest of us, just about all the way through supper. Next to her was Mr. Stacy, the hired man. On the right side, next to Aunt Alice, was "Little John," another hired hand. Next to him sat the cook, a buxom lady who always dressed in white. She was a fantastic cook.

Next to my dinner plate, and all the others, was a pie plate with an absolutely HUGE piece of lemon meringue pie. Even while we bowed our heads and Uncle Austin prayed, I couldn't take my eyes off that scrumptious looking wedge of pie. It must have stood six inches high.

I remember Aunt Alice as a kind, loving, friendly and always smiling, lady. I don't remember them having any children of their own, but she loved them. She had observed me keeping an eye on my piece of pie, so, after Uncle Austin had finished the prayer and before anything could be passed, she said, "All my life I've always eaten salad first, then meat and potatoes, and last, my dessert. Just this once, I'd like to eat my desert first. Would anybody care to join me?"

"Me! I would!" My excited response caused everybody to laugh and agree that eating our pie first sounded like a splendid idea. And, that's what we did along with a lot of friendly banter. It was superb! But do you know what? It didn't detract from the rest of the meal one tiny bit. I believe eating our dessert first made everything else taste even better.

As I finished this story I said, "And that's what we're going to do tonight. We're going to have our dessert first." Then I read the announcement that was happy information to all of us. The audience applauded lustily because of the good news and, perhaps a little bit, the story I'd told.

Now, that was a true story, in a "rosy picture" sort of a way. But, let me tell it with a slightly different twist-and without the roses.

Few people want to openly admit that their son is in prison for robbing a bank, nor that their great grandfather had been hung as a horse thief.

Right along with that, nobody wants to admit their father was a "ne'er do well." Pride would likewise prevent most of us from admitting their mother had been the "hired girl" at the County Poor Farm. I was no exception. Here's the unvarnished true story.

"Uncle" Austin wasn't really my Uncle and "Aunt" Alice wasn't really my Aunt. I just called them that. They were what's known as "shirt tail relatives." It worked like this; Uncle Charlie Miller married my Dad's sister, Mary. "Aunt" Alice was Uncle Charlie's sister. See? That's not so far fetched, is it?

Austin Merriman didn't own the farm. He managed it-for the county. The extremely big house was needed for the "indigent" who lived on the County Farm. The elevator was practically a must, because the living quarters were on the top three floors and the dining room, store rooms, laundry etc. were in the basement. And most of the homeless, but not all, were elderly and in some cases infirm. I guess that's why the County Farm was also called The County Infirmary.

The farm was well kept because all the "guests" who were able helped out to the best of their physical abilities.

Mr. Stacy was the paid hired man and Mom was the paid hired girl. That's what they were called. I think Mr. Stacy's name was Jay.

Ruth Grimm was a "guest" and, as I recall, had twin sons named Jack and Gene. She helped the cook and was sort of a maid for Aunt Alice.

"Little John" wasn't a paid hired hand. Well, not exactly. He was a permanent resident, but he wanted very much to do his share. His pay was the pocket change Uncle Austin gave him and he was allowed to eat at the "family" dining table rather than with the other residents in the main dining hall.

In truth, it was very much like one big happy family. Most of the residents had no children or any other family. The reason I say that is, for a fact, in those days families took care of "their own." It was not easy on poor folks because nobody had ever heard of food stamps or public dole. If you were down and out and your family couldn't take care of you, you went to the poor farm. It was that simple.

Well, now you know the truth, the whole truth, and nothing but the truth. Only in recent years have I had the pleasure of regularly associating with people who invariably exude and express the love and warmth I felt on the night we "had our dessert first."

10

LeRoy A. Foster — Lawyer and Poet

During a recent visit to Indiana, I was instrumental in bringing together two friends who hadn't seen each other in over 70 years. It was my first direct meeting with one of them so, it's possible, I enjoyed it as much as they did.

We all had lunch together at a charming restaurant called, simply, "The Tea Room." It's located in the Old Elkhart Hotel in Elkhart, Indiana. I heartily recommend it for your dining pleasure.

My wife, Zena, my sister, Edythe (Edie) Miller, and I arrived first. We were soon joined by Laura Lantz, whom I had written to as well as talked to by phone, and her friend, Inez Hostetler. She, too, lives in the old hotel. Inez was related to the Vanus Miller family on the Troyer side. Vanus was Edie's husband.

Edie and Laura could hardly remember each other because Edie had been a young girl and Laura a young lady when they attended the Bethel Church together.

I had gotten acquainted with Mrs. Lantz after she wrote me regarding a story I had written about her mother, Rosa Walter, and her grandmother, Olivia Merrifield. Now there were two fine ladies. I knew them both, but I never knew Laura because she had left the farm and LaGrange County in 1919—before I was born.

Since we were dining together, a logical topic of conversation seemed to be food and the differences in food between the times of our childhood and now. For instance, I chose the Broccoli Quiche for my lunch. Quiche, in case you didn't know, is a custard pie baked in a rich crust and containing various ingredients. The quiche, pronounced "keesh," that I ordered, was made with broccoli. It was absolutely delicious. Try it! You'll like it!

We were in agreement that, as children, we'd never heard of quiche and none of us could recall ever having any experience with broccoli. As a matter of fact, we'd never heard of it.

Among other foods we discussed was corn meal mush. "Poor man's porridge." Fresh made mush is usually ladled into a bowl, steaming hot, and then eaten with milk and a little sugar. It was customary to cook enough mush that enough would be left over for another meal. This left over portion would be put in a pan to cool. At supper time the firm mush could be sliced and fried. Spread with butter and syrup poured over it, fried mush is definitely pleasing to the palate. Inez Hostetler said she used to like mush and tomato gravy.

I think that's when we stopped talking about foods that we used to enjoy. Conversation kept finding its way back to the early days when Rosa Walter and my mother were close friends and members of The Bethel Ladies Aid Society. Names began to come up that I had nearly forgotten. Lynch, Springer, Krugh, Bean and some that I did know like Giggy, Bradley, Olmstead and Eaton. They spoke of Frank Olmstead and then the name Eloise Olmstead popped up.

I had talked to Eloise Olmstead Frurip on the phone and had even exchanged letters. She was the wife of Leland Frurip. Some few days after this luncheon, I had the pleasure of spending a couple of hours with Mrs. Frurip. She is a veritable jewel. Mrs. Frurip brought up the names of many of the people who I remembered. She also spoke of some who were friends of my parents.

While I visited with her, Mildred (Hart) Gitt came for a visit. She brought to mind some other names I'd forgotten.

It's nice to reminisce with old friends but, it's equally rewarding to meet new friends especially if you shared mutual acquaintances years ago.

Back to lunch at The Tea Room.

Mrs. Lantz asked if I remembered LeRoy A. Foster, lawyer and poet. I told her, "No, but I do remember a lawyer and house painter named Ralph Foster."

"Ralph was LeRoy's son. You're right, though. During the depression very few people had money to pay a lawyer. Many had to work at manual labor in order to keep food on the table. I do recall that Ralph was a good painter, too."

Mrs. Lantz continued, "LeRoy Foster was an aggressive lawyer but he had his sensitive side, too. I've brought with me a poem he wrote titled, "May." You can have it if you'd like."

I liked it and here it is:

May

Swift the humming birds are darting 'round the blooming cherry
*   trees,*
That are spilling all their nectar in the lap of every breeze,
While the droning bees, half dozing, stutter in their glad surprise
For they think they've gone to heaven through the gates of paradise;
For the wealth of all the Indies, mines of copper, silver, gold,
Are as naught to all the treasures they in ecstasy behold,
Stores of pollen, amber-tinted, founts of honey, clear and rare,
All just begging to be gathered by these reapers of the air,
And a thousand feathered songsters sing a gladsome roundelay,
For the earth is in it's Springtime, 'tis the sunny month of May.

Far above me in the treetop sits the robin in her nest,
Half asleep and sweetly dreaming of the eggs beneath her breast,
And the speckled trout, swift leaping, shines above his crystal stream,
Like a rainbow newly tinted, in an iridescent gleam.
There the heron, blue and solemn, 'neath the willow, old and bent,
Stands knee-deep amidst the rushes, half asleep and half intent
On the minnows darting past him, in the water clear and cool,
While an ever-swelling chorus rises from the distant pool
Where the pied frogs, sleek and shiny, dozing sunny hours away,
Now and then, a moment waking, join the sylvan melody.
There's a wondrous kind of beauty, in the sunshine's gleaming rays,
Just a promise of the harvest, just a hint of future days —

Bounteous days when sweet contentment walks with plenty, hand in
*   hand,*

Through the meadows, through the orchards, in fruition's promised
  land,
Where gaunt want, in somber garments, is a spectacle unknown
To the happy sprites of Summer as they dance before the throne
Where the yellow god of harvest, neath his crown of ripened grain,
Prodigal of peace and plenty, and nods and smiles again
"Till his subjects, happy-hearted, through the parting gates above
Catch a glimpse of all his splendors and they learn that he is love.

As all careless-like and lazy I lie stretched upon the grass,
As I watch the flowers nodding where the fairies' footsteps pass,
As I listen to the music throbbing through the scented air,
I can look right into heaven, see the angels smiling there;
For the angels love the sunshine as the flowers love the dew,
And I know God loves the Springtime, as He loves both Me and you,
And He wants us to be happy, just today and all the while
And He wants us to be singing and to greet Him with a smile,
So He's whispering softly to us, in His whispering kind of way,
That the pleasures that await us are just hinted of in May.

Isn't that beautiful?

Mr. Foster was making reference to the Scripture at
1 Corinthians, 2:9 which reads, "Eye has not seen and ear has not
heard, neither have there been conceived in the heart of man the
things that God has prepared for those who love him."

11

Staying Overnight With the Shrock's

No doubt I've said this before but I'm going to say it again. "Paul Shrock was my best and closest friend when I was nine." That was the year we attended Saylor School together.

There's not much use in having friends if you don't take advantage of their friendship. Now, I'm not sure that sounded the way I meant it to. What I was trying to say is, true friends want to help you when you need help.

I guess, if the facts be known, Paul was in a better position to help me than I was to help him. One thing for sure, his family always had plenty of food. The whole family worked very hard to make sure they had the proverbial "roof" over their head, clothes on their backs, and food in their stomachs.

Ed Shrock was Paul's dad. Ed had a twin whose name was Fred. I don't know exactly why I mentioned that because it's not important to my story. I just thought I'd throw it in, you know?

Ed didn't give his family much in the way of what most folks considered luxuries. He did give them one thing that's almost a luxury these day. Love. He loved his family and they knew it.

The Shrock's were plain people who didn't have much in the way of worldly goods. No excess of anything but a sufficiency of everything. Ed would have said, "We don't need to have the best to make the best of what we have."

One night, late in the fall and while we were walking home from school together, Paul asked me if I'd like to come have supper with them and stay overnight. That was the best offer I'd had in some time and I readily accepted. They had invited me to supper several times, and I had really enjoyed it, but I'd never been invited to spend the night, too. It proved to be quite an enlightenment.

I stopped at my house to leave a note for Dad, so he wouldn't worry, and the Shrock children walked on home. Not too much later I joined them. Now I had to help do chores and take care of another project Paul had known about all the time. Seems he had had an ulterior motive in asking me to stay overnight.

Fannie Shrock had emptied the straw out of every straw mattress in the house early that morning. During the day, she'd washed all the mattress covers and they had to be refilled. That's where I came in. Helping to stuff mattresses with straw. Another new experience!

The cows had to be fed and milked before supper that night. I wasn't very good at milking but I tried. Alma laughed at me because she was an experienced "milkmaid." She milked so fast and efficiently that her bucket looked like it was filling up with foam instead of milk.

I didn't get much older before I became aware that girls are lots better than boys at a goodly number of things. Admittedly, Paul was a very efficient milker, too. Only, he didn't laugh at me and my feeble efforts. Actually, Alma wasn't making fun of me. She just thought that all nine year old boys should be able to milk a cow.

Just as we finished milking and had turned the cows out, Mr. Shrock drove into the yard in his '28 Chevy. All of the kids rushed to the car and as soon as his feet touched the ground he started giving each of his children their customary hug. As a sort of afterthought, he gave me a hug, too. He probably never knew how much I needed, and appreciated, that hug.

"Well, Paul, did you get all the mattresses stuffed today?"

Seems as though he knew about this being the day to fill mattresses, too. "They're all finished and Ted helped me. We got nice clean new straw from the straw stack. I asked Ted to have supper with us tonight and to stay the night. It's all right, isn't it?"

"That's fine but, next time ask, first."

Before eating supper, we each had to wash our face and hands. A wash basin sat conveniently on a bench next to the back door. Next to the basin was an old dish with a cake of homemade soap for washing ourselves. The pump was only a few feet away making it easy to refill the basin as each user emptied his dirty water. All shared the same towel for drying.

After everybody was seated at the supper table, Mr. Shrock gave a long prayer of blessing and thanks giving. I was always impressed with his sincerity although, at the time, I'd have appreciated more brevity. He was a good man.

The supper meal almost surely was canned beef with brown gravy made from the beef drippings, which went well with boiled potatoes. Very possibly we had either canned green beans or peas, although Fannie Shrock put up a lot of dried sweet corn. We might have had both because she always tried to have something green. Everything was home canned, even the beef.

Always, there was fresh milk and homemade bread. At an Amish or Mennonite household, supper traditionally ends with pie or pudding. Believe me! That's a tradition I could get used to.

After supper, Fannie and Alma washed and dried the dishes. The living room was lighted by a lamp in the middle of a library table. Ed sat in a rocking chair next to the kerosene lamp and read the Bible.

Paul and I went upstairs to the boys bedroom. We had to put two bed ticks on the bed. That's what we called the straw-filled mattress covers. We put them back on the floor and walked on them to squish the straw down. Then we put them both back on the bed, one to sleep on, the other for a cover.

Ed and Fannie Shrock slept in a down stairs bedroom, Alma and Martha shared a bed in an upstairs room and Silas, Petey, Paul and I slept in the bed in the third bedroom.

Most likely I fell asleep thinking about the scrumptious breakfast we were going to have in the morning.

But, what a great day! What a fine friend! What a soft mattress!

And that's my memory of, "Staying Overnight with the Shrocks."

12

That Reminds Me of the Time . . .

With regularity letters come my way in which the writer remarks, "After reading your last story I said to the wife, 'That reminds me of the time . . .'" and away they go. I'd like to tell you about some of them. And, yes, ladies react in the same way.

Some excerpts from a letter written by Leta Brewer from Montgomery, Texas:

"Your Black Walnut Farm Stories bring back so many memories of my own early days and I've had many good laughs as I recall similar events.

"Especially, I remember the wooden churn. My sister and I would take turns pulling the dasher up and down while counting to one hundred.

"The radio programs! I remember our first radio as being a crystal set, made by Alfred Daniels, first announcer for KPRC. He made it so I could listen to the Democratic National Convention in Houston in 1927.

"It had to be grounded and the only place I could find was a water pipe right under my bedroom window. The connection was so short I had to sit on the floor.

"Later, we had a larger radio and all sat facing it with our eyes glued to one spot.

"I laughed about your story of The Raleigh Man. The only difference, ours was the Watkins man and he always stayed overnight at our house.

"The first plane I ever saw was down on the beach at Corpus Christi. We drove into town to see it. Our old horse decided it was too noisy and just started running, with us hanging on for dear life, until we got home about a mile out of town.

"You told a story about your Uncle's watchdogs which were guineas. Well, we had some guinea hens but my mother hated them because they would go a mile out of their way to keep us from finding their nests.

"And, you mentioned big chickens? My mother thought Buff Orpingtons were the best. My sister and I would run a marathon race to catch a chicken to fry. If we knew ahead someone was coming we caught them in the hen house, before letting them out. "The next step was to build a fire in the cook stove, summer or winter, to heat the water to scald the chicken, so the feathers would come off easy."

Then she moved away from chicken stories and brought up my story about butchering day. Different, though.

"I remember my youngest Uncle and some neighbor boys decided to kill a hog, because a Texas norther had come, while my grandmother had gone to town. Everything went well until they could not get the hog out of the scalding water. By the time they got it out it was too well done to scrape.

"My grandmother whipped my Uncle and the teenage boys with a leather strap. Their folks probably gave them some swats, also.

"On another occasion, Grandmother locked some neighbor boys in the corn shed overnight, and went and made their father come after them. No more corn ever disappeared.

"People didn't know about delinquent children and did not burden the courts. Some things were better in the old days."

I once quoted a message I took out of a fortune cookie and I'm going to do it again. Here it is:

"If your family has an old person in it, it possesses a jewel."

Leta Brewer is a jewel. Don't you agree?

While commenting on problems of discipline, Opal Gray told me a story I feel obliged to pass on.

"Uncle George and Aunt Darcus Seems had 13 children. Two girls and eleven boys. Two of the boys, Bundy and Lafey, were extremely ornery. An example of their high degree of mischievousness happened only a few days after Uncle George had bought new harnesses for his two horses.

"While they were in the barn, it struck Bundy and Lafey at the same time.

"'Let's put the harness on these two big calves and hitch them to the old hay rake! They wouldn't be able to pull the farm wagon.' And that's what they did.

"It took a lot of doin' but they eventually got the two calves harnessed and hitched to the hay rake. Not liking the idea at all, the calves took off the minute the boys stepped back from hitching the last tug.

"Neither of the boys was on the seat of the rake and so the calves were running 'free rein.' They headed straight for a tree. Instead of going around it, they split and went one on each side!

"The calves were nearly killed, the harnesses were virtually ruined, and the tongue of the old hay rack was broken.

"Aunt Darcus had heard the commotion and came outside just in time to see the conclusion.

"'What you did is worth a walloping! You've been bad! When your father comes home you tell him what you've done.'

"Here's what took place, not just this time but, every time: They knew exactly what would happen.

"When Uncle George came home he'd always sit down on the couch and take his shoes off. After he got settled real good and comfortable Bundy and Lafey would stand by the front door and tell him of their misdeeds. He'd always lose his temper, jump up, and charge after them. They'd dash out the front door with Uncle George in hot pursuit, in his stocking feet.

"Alongside the driveway was a small field that would grow nothing but a vicious plant called Mexican Sand Burs. And, since they had their shoes on, that's where the boy's headed.

"Uncle George quickly wished he hadn't followed them because his feet and socks were full of sand burs. By the time he'd picked out the sand burs and got back to the house, he was over his mad. Then he'd forget it until next time.

"Those boys sure were mischievous, to say the least." And, that's the way Opal told it.

I'm inclined to believe if my brothers and I would ever have done anything like that to our Dad we would not have escaped punishment. And, he would not have forgotten.

14

Sheep Shearing Time
at the Aaron Marker Farm

Somehow or another, I tell a lot of stories about shearing sheep during the spring of the year I was nine years old.

The reason would have to be the memories. Each farm was different and each family left me with special memories. Fortunately, the vast majority of my experiences were pleasant. And, then again, I may have blocked out the bad ones. It would be nice if we could do that all the time--remember the good times and forget the bad.

To shear sheep on the Ora Bingham farm was always a pleasure. Mrs. Bingham was taller than Ora. Tall and slender and nice to me as were all the farm women. And could she cook? You better believe it!

After dinner, they entertained us with music. Both Mr. and Mrs. Bingham were what I considered to be accomplished musicians. She played the piano and he did an excellent job with the mandolin as well as other instruments.

There was also a portable organ that they used to bring, along with the mandolin, to the Robbins Family Reunion. They were apparently related to us but I never knew in what way.

In the same neighborhood was the farm of Aaron and Madge Marker. They were good friends of Grandpa and Grandma Todd and regular sheep shearing customers of Dad's. This was to be my first year but not my last. Always before, one of my brothers went along to turn the crank of the sheep shearing rig. But, since they had all been sent to work on different farms, it was now my full time job. Without pay, of course, and none expected.

Dad got me up early and we headed for town. We needed some gas for the Model T and some oil for the shearing rig. He used heavy grease on the gears but the actual blades needed a real thin oil. The oil kept the blades from getting dull as fast as they would have otherwise. Dad had his own sharpening machine but it was still a chore to keep the blades sharp.

We bought two gallons of gas and a quart of thin oil at the DX station and started for the Marker's. No breakfast, again. I can't truthfully say I ever got used to it but the noon meal was the only meal we'd have on more days than I care to remember. It was still early when we pulled into the driveway. We drove on back to the barn and parked alongside a door that Dad knew to be the one we'd be using.

Guess what? Mr. Marker and his hired man, Francis Miller, had just finished milking. What's so special about that? They hadn't eaten breakfast yet! Mrs. Marker, Madge that is, insisted we eat with them and Dad agreed it would be all right. I could hardly wait!

Aaron and Francis took care of the milk and then cleaned up for breakfast. Just the four of us "men" took places at the table. Madge kept watch over us like a clucking mother hen. She made sure we had all we wanted to eat and then some. "You'll be working hard," she told me, "so, you'll need a good hearty breakfast."

Breakfast consisted of fresh fried potatoes, fried eggs, and sausage patties. Then, right out of the oven, biscuits with butter and strawberry jam. I had milk and the others drank coffee.

Madge was not only a good cook but I thought she was beautiful. She had real dark hair and was very light complexioned with what appeared to be very soft, smooth, skin.

In my opinion, Mr. Marker was quite a lot older than Mrs. Marker but I never knew for sure. Mr. Marker had a strange sounding voice. It was sort of high pitched and it seemed like he had to force air out his lungs in order for his voice box to work. They were a very likable couple. It made me happy when Dad later told me that they visited my Todd grandparents with some regularity. Mostly, Dad said, "They'd play cards and eat popcorn all evening." They played partner Euchre.

At that time, Grandma was pretty much "shut-in." Didn't get out of the house very much. It had been only four years since she'd been seriously injured in a head on automobile accident. Both her legs had been badly crushed and she was barely able to walk. She was always glad to have company.

But, I nearly forgot Marker's hired man. He was, perhaps, the most interesting or memorable of the three. He helped us some, while we were shearing sheep. His name was Francis Miller-but, I already said that, didn't I?

Dad complained almost every day about how much his back hurt. That wasn't hard to understand considering the strained position he had to be in while he was shearing the sheep. He was always glad of any extra help that came his way. One part of the job that seemed to take its toll on him was catching the sheep and then "wrestling" them into position so he could start shearing. That's where Francis made his contribution.

Francis worked in and around the barn most of the day as we sheared their approximately 25 head of sheep. For that reason, he was available whenever Dad needed another sheep.

First, let me tell you how Dad had to do it. He'd catch a sheep by one hind leg and pull and tug it to the shearing floor. Then, he'd grasp it behind the front legs, lift the sheep in the air, and sit it on its back side.

That was the first shearing position. After Dad got it in that position they were reasonably docile, the ewes especially. Often times, the buck sheep gave battle from start to finish. Fortunately, there was seldom more than one in a flock.

Now, let me tell you how Francis Miller caught the sheep:

Have you ever picked up a puppy by the skin on its neck? Most everybody has. Well, that's sort of what Francis did. He buried the fingers of his right hand in the wool of the sheep — it's neck — closed his hand and lifted. I promise you, his right arm was twice as big as his left! I'd never seen anything like it before, nor have I since.

The Marker's sheep were either Shropshire or Hampshire and each weighed in excess of 100 pounds. But, he'd lift each one up, with one hand, and set it down on the floor right in front of Dad. I was really impressed! He made it look easy. What a man!

I wonder what ever happened to Francis Miller.

15

Rover Takes a Short Vacation

Paul Shrock and I spent several hours together one day this past summer. Talking and talking. Our wives were there, too, but mostly they just listened. Seein' as how Paul and I hadn't seen each other since August in 1932 you'd think we'd have talked about what's happened in our lives since then. But, we didn't. Mostly, we talked about what we did at Saylor School and on his farm during the year we were both nine.

Precious moments! Everybody talks about precious moments, but it means different things to different people. In this instance, to me, it was Paul Shrock telling me stories about his mother and father. Very little about his siblings, but I hope that will come at a later time. I'd like to know about Alma and Silas. He did tell me that Petey had died at age 21.

We talked about pets and how important they are to children. Paul had a pet chicken that used to eat corn out of his hand but, over his protests, the family eventually ate the chicken. There's the problem with becoming too attached to a farm animal that may wind up on your supper plate.

Boys, especially, tend to become attached to some rather out of the ordinary pets. Like a raccoon or a frog. A frog? That reminds me! I've just got to tell you this story.

While Zena and I visited with her sister, Opal Gray, Opal's sister-in-law was visiting there, also. Her name is Virginia Bohannon and she told me a dandy story. Here it is:

Virginia's mother, Bertha Vawter, was born in 1875. She and her parents lived in a log house with a big stone fireplace in one end of the building. She remembered the big benches on each side of the fireplace.

"My mother said she'd like to have had a cat, or even a dog, but it couldn't be. Then she found this huge frog and decided to make a pet of it. The frog seemed to think it was a good idea and eventually got so it would jump into her hands when she'd hold them close to the floor. She kept it in the house."

"Hold on now," I said. "A big frog would have to be a bull frog and they need to stay close to water. It must have been a big toad."

"Maybe it was a toad. All I know is she said it was a big frog. She also told me it jumped all over the house and at night, and some times during the day, it slept in a slot where a stone had been taken out of the wall by the fireplace. The hole was close to the floor behind one of the benches.

"One day, while Mother was working in the garden, somebody left the front door open and the frog hopped out into the yard. He was hopping toward the garden where Mother was working when a big snake swallowed him down! She saw it happen!

"Quick as a flash, Mother charged the snake with hoe held on high! WHAM! WHAM! WHAM! She whacked at the snake's head with the hoe.

"She completely decapitated the snake and was able to pull the frog out still alive and none the worse for its experience!"

Just goes to show what some kids will do to protect their pets.

Now, I'll get back to what I had intended talking about in the first place: the Shrock family dog, Rover.

From my hiding place, on top of our barn, I could easily watch the comings and goings of everybody, and every thing, at the Shrock house. Rover was one of the "things" I used to watch. He was a big collie dog. At our house we had a cat named Ed, but no dog. I never believed you could teach a cat anything but, to my way of thinking, dogs were smart.

The Ed Shrock family always raised a big garden which produced fresh vegetables as well as a bountiful amount for winter consumption. Everybody in the family loved fresh vine ripened tomatoes. But, so did the chickens. Rover was taught to keep the chickens out of the garden and you should have seen him patrol. He was a true guard dog.

Rover was gentle with the children and never seemed to mind when the little ones pulled his tail or even rode on his back. However, Rover was a working dog. One of his main chores was to bring the cows up to the barn, morning and night, for milking. And this brings me to the heart of my story, "Rover takes a Short Vacation."

From my secret hiding place, I saw it happen. Ed gave the order to Rover, "Go fetch the cows!" Well, actually, he said it in Dutch. Anyway, Rover took off down the lane on the run.

Then it happened! Rover slowed down and looked over his shoulder. When he was sure they couldn't see him, he stopped and crawled through a hole in the fence. The hole was just beyond the back of our garden. With his tail between his legs, he trotted along the fence. Maybe it would be more accurate to say he was "slinking." Whatever it was, he sure appeared to be guilty, and he was. He was running away! This was a first for me. I'd seen him bring the cows up from the pasture a number of times.

After Rover was completely out of sight of the house, he stopped. Then, turning around several times like he was trampling down the tall grass, he lay down. None of the family could see him, but I could, and I didn't give him away.

When enough time had passed and the cows hadn't appeared, Mr. Shrock went to the head of the lane and commenced calling Rover. All this time, Rover tried to bury himself deeper in the tall grass. Finally, Paul was sent to fetch the cows.

The milking was all finished and the whole family was in the house eating supper when I saw Rover get up. First, he stretched real good and then started toward the house, still slinking with his tail between his legs. When he got to the back door he reached up with one paw and scratched the screen. It looked like he was knocking on the door.

Mr. Shrock was the only one who came out. Straight away, he walked over to a tree and took down a short length of rope. With his left hand he reached over and took hold of the loose skin on Rover's neck. With the rope in his right hand, he promptly flailed Rover. The dog resisted very little.

When Ed let him go, Rover ran behind the barn. After putting the rope back where he got it, Ed went back in the house to finish his supper.

Almost exactly at the time the children finished eating, Rover came back and scratched on the screen again. This time, Ed said, "Feed him." Rover was happy and so were the kids. They jumped and frolicked about, but they all got the message.

"Disobedience brings swift retribution at the Shrock house."

And, that was the end of my entertainment for the day. Besides, Dad was driving into the yard and if he caught me up on top of the barn, I'd get a sample of "swift retribution."

16

The Practical Joker
and His Bucking Bronco

Some people have a strong liking, or you might say a penchant, for playing practical jokes. Somehow, as a general rule, the perpetrator is the only one who gets any enjoyment out of their "dirty tricks." Often times, the brunt of the joke is physically injured, and without fail he suffers injury to his pride.

Have you ever seen anybody pull a chair out of the way as another person is about to sit down? That "joke" has caused more than one broken back and dozens of other injuries.

How about a dog that has been taught by its master to fetch a stick, a tennis ball, or whatever? Did you ever see some clown pretend to throw a ball for the dog to fetch and then quickly hide it behind his back? If the person is a parent, you have to wonder how he treats his children. It's actually a form of lying. Makes me think of the old saying, "You can't train a dog unless you know more than the dog."

Well, enough of that.

My brother, Lloyd, was hard to keep tied to one place. When he was in High School he stayed for a week, or maybe a month, at a number of different farm homes, then he'd start over again. Because he worked hard at whatever work or chores that needed doing, Lloyd was always welcomed. Sometimes, he was compensated with money but mostly his pay was only room and board.

Lloyd paid a number of lengthy visits to the Niles Davis, Abe Hostetler, and George Dintaman homes, but I want to talk about his stay with Roy Berry (not his real name) and his family.

Roy was married and he and his wife had children, the oldest of which was a boy about seven years old. Most of what I know about Mr. Berry are things told me by Lloyd.

For instance:

It was probably in the fall of 1931 when Lloyd and Roy were squirrel hunting that Roy's warped sense of humor first surfaced, as far as Lloyd was concerned. As they walked through the woods Roy spotted a big, red, fox squirrel scurrying up a fairly tall tree. When the squirrel stopped to look down, Roy took careful aim with his rifle and fired.

"Got 'im," he shouted.

Two problems quickly reared their ugly heads. Number one, the squirrel didn't fall to the ground as expected, but was lodged in a crotch in the tree. Dead. Number two, there were poison ivy vines growing up the trunk of the tree.

"You'll have to climb up the tree and get 'im," Roy told Lloyd. "I'm too big and, anyway, I've never been much of a climber." He was definitely a big fellow and he knew Lloyd liked to climb.

"Not me!" Lloyd answered. "I get poison ivy just by looking at it, let alone climbing a tree covered with it."

Roy tried every thing he could think of to get Lloyd to climb the tree, even ordering him to, but Lloyd still wouldn't do it. Then, Roy had an inspiration and a chance for a "practical joke."

"I'll let you use my car Saturday night."

That did it! Lloyd climbed the poison ivy covered tree and brought down the dead squirrel.

Come Saturday night, Lloyd was covered with itching, oozing, poison ivy and so miserable that he had no desire to use the car. Roy just laughed at him.

Then, there was the business with the alarm clock. Lloyd slept by himself in a double bed. On more than one occasion, Roy would set a loud alarm clock for, say, three o'clock in the morning and then hide it under the other pillow. Very funny!

And, there was the raincoat story. Inside the barn door hung an ancient raincoat that Lloyd used whenever it rained. There was an old pair of gloves in one pocket. One day, when it suddenly started to rain, Lloyd dashed into the barn and put on the old rain coat. He poked his hands into the pockets to retrieve his gloves only to find that Roy had put a generous quantity of fresh cow manure in both pockets.

"Yeck."

Bad guys always get their comeuppance. Right? Maybe this was it: Roy couldn't wait to get the Western Mare he had ordered.

During the depression, many farmers bought western horses to use for plowing and so on. They weren't quite as big as most farm horses but they were much less expensive even though they had to be shipped in from the western states. They weren't broken to plow, or to be ridden. It could have been said, these horses were purchased "as is."

Roy, and several of the younger neighbors, tried to ride this "bargain" western horse. No way would this filly allow any of them to stay on her back. She was a real, old-fashioned, bucking bronco.

"Well then, she'll have to be a plain old plow horse," Roy decided. However, he could never get her to hold still long enough to get a harness on let alone pull a plow.

"Allllll right! If you won't let anybody ride you and you won't work in harness, you'll become a brood mare. You can produce me some colts that will work!" With that, Roy took her to a neighbor who owned a stud horse. She just enjoyed it, but she didn't "take." He took her again, and again. Nothing. Talk about exasperated! Roy was fit to be tied. This mare wouldn't work, wouldn't let anybody ride her, and she apparently refused to be a "mama."

But, wait! "Why not get some laughs out of her?"

Lloyd had been watching this sleek roan mare running in the pasture. The black spots on her rump made her absolutely beautiful, to his eyes. And, could she run? She was far faster than any of the other farm horses.

Roy had been aware of Lloyd's admiration of the mare. "Tell you what I'm gonna do, Lloyd. If you can break that horse to ride, I'll let you take her to the Shipshewana race track and see how she runs against other horses."

"Now you're talkin'," Lloyd said. "I'll do it."

Grandpa Woodworth had given Lloyd a saddle. It took all his spare time and a lot of patience and sweet talk, but Lloyd eventually broke the mare to ride. She was a real "buckin' bronco" and gave Lloyd many a spill before she finally let him ride her.

The Saturday finally came when Lloyd was going to the horse races. I was there. I had walked from our house to Roy Berry's

Lloyd Woodworth

farm hoping to talk Lloyd into letting me go to Shipshewana with him. Eventually, he agreed.

"One thing, Ted. When you climb on behind me, DO NOT accidentally kick her in the ribs!"

Lloyd maneuvered the horse alongside the horse tank, which I was standing on, and I climbed aboard, quickly putting my arms around Lloyd's waist. Somehow, without meaning to, I let one of my heels touch the horse's ribs.

Wow! I'd seen a bronco bucking before, but never while I was on it. Talk about something fierce and bone-wracking! She would just kick viciously for a while then she'd seem to spring into the air and come down on all four feet. What a jolt! Then she'd spin around and around, all the time trying to bite us.

Lloyd finally got her to running and she started down the road to Shipshewana as hard as she could go. When she eventually tired and slowed down to a walk, Lloyd expressed his unhappiness with me.

About half way to the race track, one of Lloyd's friends pulled up beside us in his car. Lloyd told him about the bucking experience we'd had.

The friend said, "I'm going to Shipshewana, too. Ted, I'll buy you an ice cream cone when I get there if you'll do something for me."

"What? What do you want me to do?" At that time in my life I'd have done almost anything to get an ice cream cone.

"Kick the horse in the ribs!" and I did.

You know what happened.

Lloyd was *really* unhappy with me, and you know what? I don't remember ever getting the ice cream cone I was promised.

So, practical jokes are never rewarding, and usually, somebody gets hurt one way or another.

17

The Wedding and the Shivaree

My sister, Edythe, graduated from Shipshewana High School in the year 1928. During the eight years she attended the one room school called Green and her four years at "Shipshe," Vanus Miller was one of her classmates. It would be fair to say, "they saw a lot of each other while they were growing up." As a matter of fact, they lived within a mile of each other all during this time.

Vanus was better than average at almost everything he did. He was a good student, popular with the boys and girls, and on top of that, he was handsome. Two of his favorite sports were baseball and basketball, and he was as good, or better, than any of the other boys at both. He was strong, well built, and definitely athletically inclined.

During his senior year, Vanus was class president. Guess who was vice-president? Edie Woodworth was class vice-president. Should it have come as a big surprise when they were married three years later? Maybe it wasn't that they got married so much as it was the way they did it.

Dad and I lived in the parsonage of the Church. Mom and my brothers did too, whenever they were home. But, did Vanus and Edie get married in the Church with everybody there, all dressed up and watching? Did I get to see them get married? No! Did Mom and Dad and my brothers see it? No! But, did my sister Mary see it? Yes! She and her husband, Truman Oesch, were the only witnesses as the Bethel preacher, George Grantham, performed the ceremony at his farm home.

Dad was fit to be tied. "I declare! I don't know what this generation is coming to. Run off and get married! Why didn't they get married in the Church, proper?"

"Oh, shaw! Count your blessings, Pa! If they'd had a big Church wedding the bride's father would have had to foot the bill. That means you!"

"Well, but, now, uh, I couldn't have paid for it." Dad was seeing the situation from an entirely different angle.

"I know that and so did they. Don't you see? They were just trying to help you save face." Ma wasn't exactly happy about the arrangement but, at least, she had known about it.

Mom and Edie didn't keep many secrets from each other. They were always very close, not that Mom and Mary weren't, too. Maybe the fact that Edie was born on Mom's nineteenth birthday had something to do with their closeness. My mother always looked younger than her actual age and by the time Edie was twenty they looked more like sisters than mother and daughter. And even more so, in later years. That made Mom very happy but I'm not sure my sister felt the same.

Arrangements were being made for Vanus to take over operation of his Grandmother Troyer's farm right near Rainbow Lake. But, in the meantime, Vanus and Edie would be staying with his parents, Ed and Barbara Miller. And that's where it happened! SHIVAREE! About three days after the wedding, and near midnight, neighbors and friends of the newly married couple came to perform the customary mock serenade to a newly married couple.

Below the window of their second story bedroom, the shivaree, or belling, began. Such an unusual racket you've never heard. I heard it. I was there! Someone had a cowbell and another a set of sleigh bells. I guess that's the reason some call this tradition a "belling."

Most everybody had some kind of noisemaker. There were horns and whistles as well as people beating on old pots and pans.

Car horns? Oh, Yes! There were car horns. I suppose the most noisome was the horn from Chester and Nellie Wurtsbaugh's shiny black Model A Ford. After all this noise-making had awakened the entire household, Vanus and Edie came out to greet the revelers. Knowing this was going to happen, Vanus had purchased a box of cigars to distribute among the men and enough candy bars for the children and ladies. That in itself was a real treat for me. I didn't get that many candy bars.

When things got quieted down a bit, the bride and groom were loaded onto a spring wagon and the parade began. Tin cans had been tied to long strings and attached to the back of the wagon so they would clatter along the ground as the wagon was briskly pulled by a spirited team of horses.

The outfit was, I think, furnished and driven by Virgil and Virginia Schutt.

The rest of the caravan was all automobiles.

Truman and Mary had come from Topeka, Merril and Vera Eaton had brought my brother Charles. Lloyd was there and he had brought me. Believe it or not, Dad had let him drive the Model T.

All the Foltz boys were there. Bill, Reuben, Roy, Grandville and Byron. Rueben especially enjoyed something like a belling. John Robert, Margaret, and Mary Ann Doney came with Orene Anderson.

Harry Hart wouldn't have missed it for anything and there were more — many more.

The procession headed east with the spring wagon and its special occupants in the lead. On past the farm where we had lived until a couple of months before. Then to the Foltz farm where we turned back right to follow alongside the Black Walnut Farm. Nettie and George Doney heard us coming, as did everybody else on our route, and they came out to cheer us on. We turned right again, between Green School and Grandma Woodworth's farm. Next we passed Wellington Bradley's and Charlie Gushwa's. I can't remember but, probably, the whole Bradley clan came out if only to see what was going on. Quite possibly, Dorothy, Margaret, Tom, and Paul were with us.

Next we made another right and passed "Toot" Frisbeys farm. Audra and Roger were likely with us, too. Then a left turn, taking us back to Millers. Then, everybody headed for home. Happy!

Total distance traveled? About four miles.

Total memories for all of us? A jillion.

The Wedding Couple
Vanus Miller and Edythe Woodworth

18

The Piano Playing Coal Deliveryman

Living in the parsonage of the Bethel Church had its advantages. For instance, just sitting in a pew doesn't actually give one much opportunity to really look at or explore a church. When it's empty—that's the best time.

Dad was not the minister at the church—far from it—but, he had a key. Wait! You know what? I'm not sure he had a key. I don't think there was a key. The more I think of it the more I doubt the church was ever locked. And, why would it be locked? In those days people had respect for what was considered to be "God's House." Rather than steal something it was more likely a passer-by would step in and leave something in the ever-present collection plate.

What I do remember was that we were supposed to clean the church and the yard. Dad had made a deal to do this in order to help us pay the rent. Our rent was $3.00, that's *three* dollars, a month, and more likely than not Dad didn't have it when it came time to pay.

The church had a full basement that included a furnace and coal room as well as one really big room that was built to allow for church socials. I don't mind telling you, I was always glad when the Ladies Aid Society had one of their socials. There was always an abundance of food, and the ladies furnished all. A "free will" offering was taken and the money given to the secretary-treasurer of the church. I took advantage of the "free" part of the free will offering. I never had any money and Dad didn't ever attend. More than once, the kind ladies would give me some of the left over food to take home with me. It was most welcome and I let them know how much I appreciated it.

The furnace was something that caught my attention. It was the first one I had ever seen and I remember wishing for winter to come so I could see how it operated. I later found out that it worked very well and, on at least one occasion, it worked too well when I overloaded it with coal. The church was so hot on that Sunday, the men all took off their coats and the windows and doors had to be opened.

Each of the leaded, stained glass, windows were just crying out for a little boy's close inspection, I thought.

And I didn't disappoint them for I spent hours looking at the different colored glass shapes. I speculated on how they colored the glass the way they did. Finally, I decided they had mixed dye with the sand. I had heard, or read, that glass was made by melting sand. Maybe I was at least close.

The ceilings were very high but, then, aren't they high in all churches? Maybe that's why people tend to speak softly when they talk or when they sing.

And speaking of singing, I loved to sing. There was this time- but, let me tell you about it.

There were little topless boxes on the back of each pew wide enough to hold two hymnals. On this occasion when the church was empty, I had helped myself to one of those books and had stationed myself behind the pulpit. With the song book opened up to "Up From The Grave He Arose," I laid it on the pulpit and, standing on my tiptoes in order to see, I began to sing.

Low in the grave He lay, Jesus my Savior
Waiting the coming day, Jesus my Lord

(Those words were sung low and sad. Then the chorus started with even lower notes. Soon, however, the music built up to a virtual crescendo of joyous sound. I loved it!)

Up from the grave he arose With a mighty triumph o'er his foes.
He arose a victor from the dark domain
And he lives forever with his Saints to reign.
He arose! He arose!
Hallelujah! Christ arose!

At that precise moment the front door was flung open and two men were standing in the doorway, exuberantly applauding. I was really startled and didn't know whether I should be worried at being caught or to be happy because they were both clapping their hands.

The sun was to their backs and I couldn't tell who it was until "Bravo! Bravo, Teddy Boy! That was very good. But, you'd sound even better with an accompaniment. Let me play the piano for you while you sing," and he loudly strode toward the piano.

Only then did I realize it was Vanus Miller and William "Bill" Foltz. Vanus sometimes played the piano on Sunday at the church. He also was sweet on my sister Edie. "You stay right up there and sing the verses and Bill and I will join in on the chorus. Ready?"

And that's what we did. How happy I was that they had taken out even a little of their time to pay attention to me. They were both having a good time, too, freely singing out. The three of us veritably filled the church with music.

When the song was finished, Vanus got up from the organ stool and said, "Well done, Teddy Boy. But, Bill and I have to get back to work." After they had tromped noisily to the front door, Vanus turned and almost shouted, "Hallelujah!" And out the door they went.

It was a long time before I found out that "Hallelujah" meant Praise Jah and Jah was a shortened form of God's name, Jehovah.

As it happened, Vanus and Bill had brought a load of coal to off load into the church basement. I hadn't heard them drive up so they had stood at the front door listening to me entertain myself by singing in the church, at the top of my lungs.

They never told the preacher about what I had done and I never told the preacher about "The Piano Playing Coal Deliveryman.

19

The Inventor's Wife

At the LaGrange High School Alumni Banquet I met a slew of people I hadn't seen in years. Zena and I sat at a table with Bob Smith from St. Charles, Missouri. He and I graduated from High School together in 1940. There were others of our class there too, but not many. I remember talking to John Fisher, "Casey" Jones, um—uh—you know? That's all. No! Wait! Don and Betty Miller came in after the excellent meal had been served. But, that's all of my graduating class I remember seeing. However, there was a big crowd considering the last class was graduated in 1964 and 50 students would have been considered a large class.

I met so many people that I don't remember them all and I'm sorry. Robert Armstrong—with a goatee—and his sister, Elmira Eberly, were there. Their mother, Alice, used to give readings at the Robbins Family Reunion. I never have found out how the Armstrongs and Robbins, or Woodworth's, are related.

Robbins Family! Yes! Willowdeane (Robbins) Austin was there! Such a joy and surprise to see her. It's been at least 40 years since we last attended a reunion together.

We're family, you know. Her father and my father were first cousins. That makes us—what?—fourth cousins? Anyway, we're kinfolks.

Back in The Good Old Days family ties were stronger. But then, we weren't such a mobile society. In other words, it wasn't so unhandy for us to get together.

I'm having a nostalgia attack!

We had an abundance of talent in the Robbins-Woodworth family. Singers, story tellers, players of various musical instruments—you name it—we had it.

My sister, Edie Miller, sent me a poem I think you'll enjoy. It was one of my mother's favorites and she recited it more than once at our reunions. Here it is:

The Inventor's Wife

It's easy to talk of the patience of Job,
Well, Job had nothin' to try him.
If he'd a been married to Johnathan Brown,
Folks wouldn't have dared to come nigh him.
Trials, indeed! Now, I'll tell you what,
If you want to be sick of your life,
Just come and change places with me a spell,
For I'm an inventors wife.

And, such inventions,
Why really, I'm never quite sure when I pick up my coffee pot,
That John ain't been trying to improve on it,
And it may'nt go off like a shot.
Why, didn't he make me a cradle once that would keep itself a
*   rockin'?*
And didn't it pitch the baby out, an' wasn't his head bruised
*   shockin'?*
And there was his patent peeler, too. A wonderful thing I'll say!
But, it never stopped, just peeled and peeled, 'till the apple was all
*   peeled away.*

When John and I kept company, he weren't like this you know,
My folks thought he was dreadful smart, but that was years ago.
He was handsome as a picture then, and he had such a glib bright
*   way,*
I never thought a time would come that I'd rue my wedding day.
But when I've been forced to chop the wood and tend to the yard
*   besides,*
And look at John a sittin' there, I've just dropped down and cried

We lost the hull of our turnip crop, while he was inventin' a gun.

I counted that one of those miracles when it burst before he was done.

So, he turned it into a burglar alarm, it ought to give thieves afright,

It would scare an honest man out of his wits, if he'd sot it off at night.

Sometimes I wonder if John isn't crazy,

He does such curious things.

Have I told you about his bedstead yet? It was full of wheels and springs.

And it had a key to wind it up and a clock face at the head,

And all you did was turn them hands and at any time you said,

That bed got up and shook itself and bounced you on the floor,

And then shut up just like a trap so you couldn't sleep any more.

Well, John he fixed it all complete and he set it for half-past five,

But he hadn't more than got into it when, dear me sakes alive!

That bed began to whizz and whirr and I heard a dreadful snap,

And there was that bedstead with John inside, shut up jest like a trap.

I screamed of course but it weren't no use

And I worked that hull long night,

Trying to open that durn fool thing, 'til at last I got in a fright.

I couldn't hear his voice inside, and I thot he might be dying,

So I took a crowbar and smashed it in. There was John peacefully lyin',

Trying to invent a way to get out again.

That was all very well to say,

But I don't think he'd a found that out if I'd left him in all day.

Now, since I've told you my story,

Do you wonder I'm tired of life? Or think it strange I often wish

I weren't an inventors wife?

20

The Rigbys from Kentucky

When Chester Rigsby was in the first grade at Saylor school, he was as bald as a billiard ball. Not a hair on his head! He looked like a miniature "Curley," as in "The Three Stooges." 'Course, the Three Stooges weren't around yet in 1932. And, Chester was twice as tough as "Curley" ever thought of being.

Chester's head wasn't shaved, so he couldn't be judged as being truly bald, it was just that his grandmother cut his hair so short he looked bald. There sure wasn't enough hair to part. Chester never had to worry about washing his hair, he just had more face to wash than other young 'uns.

There were a number of advantages to such a hair cut. One thing for sure, nobody could pull his hair nor could they run their fingers through it. "Rock headed!" That's what Miss Neely said he was. "Rock headed!" For a fact, Chester had the hardest head of anybody I ever met. Man or boy. His head was so hard he used it for a battering ram. That kept him in trouble a fair amount of the time.

In all fairness to Chester, it was his older brother, Jim, who would more likely than not be the instigator whenever Chester got into a fight of any kind. For example; If Jim was involved in any kind of an altercation that he was afraid he couldn't handle, he'd call for Chester. That was almost like sicking a mean bulldog on somebody. The difference was, Chester would come at the other boy head down like a charging buck-sheep or maybe a billy goat, and WHAM! He'd hit the boy, with his hard head, somewhere between the knees and the stomach, depending on how tall the other boy was. It hurt! I know it hurt! He "butted" me more than once.

Jim won almost all of his school yard fracases in that manner.

Eventually, everybody from the first to the eighth grade learned not to pick on Jim or Chester Rigsby.

There was a reason why the Rigsby boys felt a need to protect and take care of each other. It seems their mother had died when Chester was only nine weeks old. Just a baby. When their father reached the point where he couldn't handle the responsibility of their care he sent them to live with their maternal grandmother in Indiana. Her name was Sarah Carroll. I met her only once, that I can remember. Let me tell you about that meeting. It's one of the favorite jewels that has been stored in my memory bank all these years.

Dad never said very much about it, but he didn't like it when I failed to come directly home from school. I never worried much about what I now realize was his genuine concern for my well-being, because he was seldom there when I got home from school. So, being alone, there didn't seem to be a whole lot for me to do. I can't remember Miss Neely ever assigning us much homework, nor can I remember having any toys to play with. One recourse was to go to some other boy's house after school let out. And, that's how I met Grandma Carroll.

The farm, where they lived, was a little bit south and east of Saylor School. That was pretty much in the opposite direction of where I lived. No matter! When the Rigsby boys asked me to walk home with them, I agreed. I'd have done it anyway, but Jim added a tempting inducement. Cornbread! "Grandma almost always has some fresh baked cornbread and a cup of milk ready for us when we get home."

Jim's words were music to my ears. I followed him home as though he were the "Pied Piper of Hamelin." Food! That was the magic word. I could never get enough and cornbread sounded good to me.

Typical boys, we played on the way to their house. The road was gravel so there were lots of rocks the right size for throwing. Boys can always find something to throw a rock at or they'll try to see who can throw a rock the farthest or the highest. We didn't really waste a lot of time getting to their farm and when we got there we headed straight to the kitchen door.

"Wipe your feet on that gunny sack and don't let any flies in with you!" It was their grandmother giving us all grandmotherly orders. She wasn't finished. "And, don't go settin' down at the table 'til you've washed your hands. I saw you a comin' so I set out three bowls of cornbread." Actually, it was a whole square pan of corn bread with three empty bowls and a pitcher of milk.

"Who's your young friend?"

Jim hadn't really had time to introduce me to her. She hadn't stopped talking since the time we hit the screen door. His grandma had never seen me before, nor I her.

It was love at first sight! On my part, at least. She'd just baked the cornbread and I loved her for it. She was thin and grandmotherly looking. I remember thinking her flowered dress had probably been real pretty when it was new, but now it was faded and old. And, of course, she wore an apron that tied in the back.

Although Grandma Carroll scolded and fussed at us, she did it with a twinkle in her eyes that couldn't mask her love of these boys. I thought it was just great and I enjoyed every minute of it.

In no way can I describe her Kentucky accent. It sounded different than Leroy and Ray Combs sounded. The Combs family originated from deep within the Kentucky hills. I knew only that Mrs. Carroll and the boys were from Kentucky and I liked their accent.

When Grandma Carroll shooed us out of the house she did it literally. She took hold of the sides of her apron and waved it at us as we went out the back door. Jim and Chester had to "see to" the livestock. There wasn't that much of it, but it had to be seen to. As I recall, there was a Jersey cow, a couple of pigs and some chickens. The boys needed to be taught responsibility, therefore they tended the farm animals. It was their job. Their chores.

The old farm house was covered with stucco and the doors and trim needed painting. The barn was red but could have soaked up a couple more coats of paint without any problem. During the depression it wasn't at all unusual to find farm buildings in need of paint. Many were weather beaten, to put it mildly.

My visit with the Rigsby boys must have been in the spring, because I remember there being a garden. Peas were up and thick. There were neat rows of sweet corn and a row of lettuce. Humongous potato plants that looked like they'd make a dozen big potatoes to the hill. Tall plants with big leaves? "What vegetable is that?" I asked Jim.

"Those are tobacco plants," he answered.

Another first. I'd never seen them before.

Later, when I told Dad about it, he said, "It's probably against the law but I say it's none of the law's business."

Then, I discovered why they raised the tobacco. Grandma Carroll was coming out of the house to see what we were doing in the garden. Much to my surprise, she was smoking a pipe! A clay pipe!

That, too, was another first.

21

"Pete, The Berry Picker," and His Friend, "Little John"

Truly, I feel a signal pleasure when someone lights up the dark recesses of my memory bank. An enlightenment, you might say. I need it regularly. In a recent story I said, "Nobody ever told me who built the 'house of many rooms' called the County Farm or when it had been built." "Why?" was another question. "Was it an oversized private home or had it been built to house indigent residents of LaGrange County?"

A letter from Charles Olds supplied me with some of the answers. Here's what he told me:

The "County Infirmary" was built June 1882 by the P. N. Stroup Lumber Co. of LaGrange. The total cost of construction was $8,768.19. He opined the $0.19 was tax.

To quote Mr. Olds, "The old windmill building is still there. I have very good observance of the fruit cellar from the top side. It is now a ground hog haven. In a picture I have there appears to be some small buildings near, which aren't any more." Mr. Olds also commented that he had attended Huff's Corner School for eight years. Having been born in 1909, he has seen "quite a change."

One of the residents of the County Farm was a man known simply as "Little John." He was one who was down and out financially but prided himself on his physical abilities, considering his diminutive size. I'm just sure he wasn't over five feet tall and couldn't have weighed more than 100 pounds. His clothes looked like they had come from the children's section of the department store. They could have, too, except they were furnished by the county.

Somehow, his dark blue, bib, overalls and his long sleeved, light blue, shirt never seemed to get dirty. His clothes were washed and ironed by the lady inmates of the County Farm. He just prided himself on staying clean no matter how dirty the work was that he was engaged in.

"Little John" worked in the dairy barn right alongside Jay Stacy, the hired man. He also handled the horses as well as a much bigger man without any problems. He plowed with a team, cultivated, made hay, and did just whatever had to be done. But, since he wasn't a regular employee, he didn't get paid except for the pocket change Austin Merriman used to give him. On the other hand, he got his room and clothing and as an added privilege, he was allowed to eat his "three square meals a day" at the "family" dining table rather than with the other residents in the dining hall. "Little John" definitely wanted to pay his own way and he did.

An unlikely friend of his was another resident that I recall was known simply as, "Pete" or "Pete, the berry picker." He, as well as Little John, must have had another name but I never knew what it was. He had more trouble keeping clean, doing nothing, than did Little John working industriously all the time.

"Pete" just never appeared to be clean. He was a very thin man and he squatted a lot. That made his pant knees always look baggy. On top of that, because he was so thin, his overalls were too big for him. The County Farm supply of clothes must have been something like the army. There weren't any special made clothes for unusual-shaped people.

Pete insisted on wearing flannel shirts the year round and, since the County Farm didn't furnish deodorant in those days, he tended to smell a little "ripe" during the summer months. They did have Lifebuoy soap, I believe, but Pete didn't indulge himself with a bath, at least not regularly.

Pete used to sit, or stand, with his arms folded inside his overalls. For convenience, he didn't button the two buttons on each side of his overalls. It appeared as though he didn't have any arms.

He didn't have any teeth, and that's a fact. Even so, he chewed tobacco! Furnished by the county! Since he didn't customarily shave more than once a week, the tobacco juice tended to cling to his stubble of whiskers as it dribbled from the corners of his mouth. That helped make him look and smell, uh, less than desirable.

His hat! An old, decrepit, shapeless, black, felt hat that must have been some kind of a security blanket type thing to him. I say that because he wore it constantly. Honestly, I'd not have been surprised to find he'd purloined it from some watermelon patch scarecrow.

You know something? Pete looked very much like a scarecrow, himself. Pete had his good points, though. In the spring, Pete was one of the most successful mushroom hunters around. Ralph Terry, who ran Terry's Meat Market, used to pay him a dollar a pound for all he brought in. Ralph used to re-sell some of them, but I think he took most of them home to enjoy eating them himself. And I can appreciate that.

Pete had another attribute. He knew how to find, and how to pick, wild black raspberries. He had these wooden quart berry boxes stashed away, somewhere, all winter long. Come berry picking time in the spring, "Pete the berry picker" sallied forth and started making his paths in the woods across the road from the County Farm. Paths through the berry bushes.

Pete might have been a bit slow of wit in a host of ways but he knew how to market wild, black, raspberries.

The berries started ripening on the top of the bushes, first. After a time the berries underneath, or away from the sun, would ripen. Pete had discerned that the berries underneath were larger, but not as plentiful.

Therefore, Pete would fill the box nearly full with the smaller berries that had been nearer the sun. Then, he'd top the box off with the larger berries which grew underneath.

Pete would sell his berries door to door. He only got $0.05 a quart for his wild black raspberries, but it gave him jingling money for his pockets and that made him feel worthwhile and at least a little independent.

Everybody needs to have a feeling of dignity as well as pride.

22

The "Niley" Davis Family

My brother, Lloyd, counted Keith Davis as one of his best friends. Keith was the oldest of the three sons of Niles "Niley" Davis. Steward was next and Maurice was the youngest. Esther and Doris were the two sisters, both older than the boys. There's an interesting story told about Keith when he was six, according to Esther who is now Mrs. Robert English.

The Davis clan considered babies to be "Good News." For that reason, when Maurice was born, six year old Keith strutted around proudly saying over and over, "Three boys. Three boys." Doris and Esther, aged nine and ten, decided to compose a jingle, and here it is:

What are we so happy about?
Look in the bedroom and you'll find out.
A tiny baby brother
In the bed with mother.

Niles, and his wife Ida, had reason to be proud of their five "Good News." Those five children, taking a cue from their school teacher parents, each wound up with a super good education. What did they do with it? They put it to good use by sharing it with others. Passed it on, you might say. Cumulative, they had over 170 years of teaching service.

Now, many of their children are teachers.

Maybe it wasn't good enough for Ripley's "Believe it or Not" but something mighty spectacular happened in 1954. That was the year the three Davis brothers, Keith, Steward, and Maurice, were coaches at High Schools in three adjoining counties. Now, you'd have to admit something like that wouldn't happen just every day.

But, guess what? Their schools each won their respective counties basketball tournaments. That's quite a feat. It's small wonder the three received national attention.

The children of this remarkable family of school teachers are making their parents proud. They are another generation of super-achievers including at least one doctor, lawyer, nurse, farmer, businessman and other professional people. All have "pleasured" their parents.

The Davis family roots go back a long way, but the Davis' Northern Indiana roots began in Shipshewana when Hezekiah's wife, Sarah, suggested the community be named after a Pottawattomi Indian, Chief Ship-she-wah-no. How about that? And, he's buried on the shores of Lake Shipshewana. Hezekiah and Sarah had a son Eugene. He and his wife, Alice, had ten children.

Right now I'm going to stop and say that I knew Alice Davis. My brother, Wayne, worked for her for at least two years while he went to school in Shipshewana. Memories are swirling through my mind about her and her house.

She was thin and I thought she was old when I knew her. But, she had beautiful furniture and served good meals. I remember a nighttime snack of chocolate covered graham crackers. I'd never seen them before. Somehow, I vaguely remember a girl named Yvonne-Hostetler-I think. She was the most beautiful girl I'd ever seen. Memories . . .

My brother loved Mrs. Davis. She was very good to him.

Here's another memory. One of Niley's brothers was named Geney. Probably his name was Eugene, Junior. All of the Davis's I knew were relatively tall. Not Geney. But his wife was tall. I remember Geney as an extremely hard working farmer, with his wife doing a man's days work right along side him.

Lest I forget, on one of my infrequent visits to the Niley Davis home, Steward and Maurice and I built several snow men, as well as a snow fort. Wayne was there, too. It was during the winter, of course, and he was staying with Alice Davis. We really had a fun time although the purpose of building the fort was to hide behind it and throw snowballs at the ones out in the open. Just good clean fun. Right?

Wayne had always been one of the best snowball packers and throwers I'd ever seen when we went to Green School. Now, I was witnessing his meeting his match if not his master. Steward was some kind of a snowball thrower. He threw hard and unbelievably accurate. He and Wayne ended up throwing at each other and Maurice and I mostly just watched them.

All three of the boys turned out to be first class ball players, both baseball and basketball. Niley liked to play ball, too. However, he was missing the thumb and first finger on his mitt hand. Used to carry that hand in his pocket most of the time-when he wasn't playing ball.

Niley was a farmer, along with all the other things he did. He wanted his children to get an education so bad, he mortgaged his farm in order for three of them to attend college.

One of the ten children of Eugene and Alice Davis was named Pearl. Pearl married a man named Jay Conrad. He was my Great Uncle. Let me explain that.

On my mother's side of the family, my great grandfather's name was Stephen Reynolds. My great grandmother's maiden name was Sarah Cleveland. It's not dreadfully important to this story but, since I have this information, her father's name was Peter Cleveland and her mother's maiden name was Susan Nelson.

Anyway, Stephen and Sarah Reynolds had a daughter they named Edith. They may have had more children. I just don't know. She was my Grandmother and the mother of Sylvia Pearl Todd Woodworth. Great-grandfather, Stephen, died and subsequently Great-grandmother, Sarah, married Houston Conrad. They had a son whose name was Jay Conrad. He married Pearl Davis. They had a son whom they named Marion, and his daughter is Donna Anchell.

Whewww!

Do you see where this story is leading? I'm attempting to claim blood relationship to the prestigious Davis family of Shipshewana.

Can you blame me?

23

Spying on our Neighbors, The Ed Shrock Family

From my lookout spot on the barn roof, I could watch the comings and goings of the neighbors. They never knew I watched them with some regularity. Not only was I able to see them clearly but I could hear them plainly.

The small field that separated our houses was lower than the land on which the houses stood. Kind of like a hollow, you might say. Whatever you called it, it created something like an amphitheater effect. The acoustics were such that I could hear everything said while they were in the back yard. When they were in the house, I couldn't hear a thing. I could hear, when they were in the back yard, but I couldn't understand. They always spoke in Dutch.

Rover, the Shrock family dog, could understand Dutch but he couldn't speak it. Kind of like it worked out with me, later on. I could hear him whine or bark and he sounded just like an English dog. The chickens clucked and chatted, in English I remember thinking, while they scratched in the driveway looking for small pebbles to fill their gizzards.

It wasn't until five years later, in 1936, that I heartily wished I had tried harder to learn to talk what is still known as "Pennsylvania Dutch." The Shrocks were Mennonites and their first language was Dutch. Their second language was English.

Let me stop right here and tell you a little about the history and beliefs of the Mennonite religion, in case you don't already know.

The first Mennonites belonged to a church organized in Zurich, Switzerland, in 1525. They were called Swiss Brethren. They believed that the choice to become a believer can only be made by an adult, and so they baptized only those adults who made that choice. They were nicknamed "Anabaptists" which means re-baptized. It was an appropriate name since those adult believers had all been baptized as infants. The name "Mennonite" came from Menno Simons who led the Anabaptists in the Netherlands and Northern Germany in the 1530's. The Mennonites later split into groups, including the Amish.

Mennonites base their beliefs on the Bible, especially the New Testament. Their "creed" is the Sermon On The Mount, found in the Bible book of Matthew, Chapters 5 through 7. Mennonites believe, among other things, that the Bible teaches that believers should be peacemakers, and therefore cannot go to war or engage in violence of any kind.

Swiss Mennonites left Europe because of persecution, and moved to Pennsylvania in 1683 after William Penn offered them religious freedom. There now are many branches of Mennonites. Some still live in rural areas, but increasingly more have moved to cities and urban settings. The Pennsylvania Dutch dialect is fast disappearing from Mennonite life and culture.

Back to the Shrocks.

In addition to running a farm, Ed Shrock had another job which kept him away from home until five in the evening or later. That was my favorite time to be in my secret spy location.

The Shrock family car was a 1928, four door, box shaped, disc wheeled, Chevrolet. The spare tire and wheel were mounted on the back between or above the bumpers. I thought it was a magnificent automobile and I was enraptured by the way Mr. Shrock would turn into the driveway without seeming to slow down from his road speed. He'd done it so many times the entry was nothing but a bank of gravel with two wide tracks in it. When he got just beyond the back of the house he'd stop in a cloud of dust. All the children were there to meet him and get a hug. How I envied them. Fannie Shrock would be in the kitchen putting the finishing touches on supper. After Mr. Shrock had made sure everybody had gotten a hug he'd pull out his big red bandanna handkerchief and help "Petey" blow his nose. He always had a cold—Petey, I mean.

If, by some chance, Paul hadn't seen to it that the cows were in the barnyard Mr. Shrock would order Rover to go fetch them. That gave everybody time to eat supper.

After they'd eaten, it was time for milking. Early morning until dark, or later, the work on the farm was never ending. From the time the children got home from school and changed clothes, there were chores to do.

In the summertime, when many children spent their time at fun and games, farm kids helped with whatever work there was to do. This included helping plant and care for a garden. And then there was canning time. Mostly, the girls helped with the canning along with learning to cook, wash and iron clothes-how to be homemakers. And the boys? Mostly they learned how to farm.

All this work was done in six days. Only the milking and the barest of chores were done on Sunday. But cooking? Of course! The Mennonite religion taught that at least part of the Old Mosaic Law was still in effect. Such as, literally, "Remember the Sabbath to keep it holy." No work except caring for livestock that could not take care of themselves. No buying, no selling, no trading.

Times change. Understanding the scriptures grows brighter as the end draws near. Proverbs 4:18 says, "But the path of the righteous ones is like the bright light that is getting lighter and lighter until the day is firmly established."

Maybe the Mennonite religion has changed—some. One Sunday, Dad sent me over to the Shrocks to buy two quarts of milk. He had given me a dime and a clean two quart fruit jar, to put the milk in. Five cents a quart was the going price, then.

The Shrocks were finished with the morning milking and were assembled at the breakfast table when I knocked on the kitchen door.

"Come in!" Mr. Shrock called out, and I did. Doors were seldom locked unless just to keep them closed.

"Dad wants to know if he can buy two quarts of milk. He sent ten cents." I held out the ten cent piece and the fruit jar, complete with sealing rubber and zinc lid.

"Get the boy a jar of milk, Alma." I was sure Mr. Shrock was displeased with me for interrupting his breakfast. But, not so. There was another reason.

When Alma brought me the milk, Mr. Shrock said, "There's your milk, Ted. Tell your father it's a gift. We don't buy or sell on Sunday, nor will we deprive anybody of food if we can help it."

With that, he handed me back the ten cent coin and Alma handed me the milk. I took the milk and, looking at Mr. Shrock, I said, "Thank you! Thank you very much!" Then, as I went out the back door, I turned and again said, "Thank you."

Until that minute I'm sure Mr. Shrock hadn't appreciated just how poor our family was. The bottle of milk meant a lot to us.

When I gave the half gallon of milk and the dime to Dad he was mystified. When I explained what had happened, he said, "Well, I declare! There are some good people left in the world after all. I hope you thanked him properly."

I'm pretty sure I had.

1928 CHEVROLET, Imperial Landau

24

I Remember Cecil Christler's Geese

Alonzo Turner said to me, "How'd you and Zena like to join Darla and me in destroying about five big pizzas come Sunday night? We're inviting some mutual friends and the pizza joint will deliver. Just bring your appetite. What do you say?"

"Sounds like you've made me an offer I can't refuse. I've never heard it put quite like that. Destroy pizza. No doubt about it, that's the kind of destruction derby I'd like to be part of." Alonzo's a man after my own heart.

Turned out that the five size "huge" pizzas, loaded with an assortment of toppings, was only part of the "spread." There was green salad, spaghetti and meat sauce, Texas style beans, nachos and on and on. Like I said, "It's the kind of destruction derby I like to get involved in." We didn't "destroy" it all, but we made an appreciable dent in it.

There were "twenty plus" people there. During dinner, and afterward, we listened to music, told stories, and played games. Naturally, I latched onto one of the stories and I want you to hear it. Truthfully, it wasn't the only good story told but, somehow, this story brought back a memory that has troubled me since I was nine years old. I'll tell you what that memory was.

But first, let me tell you the story Kenneth Reed told us at the party.

"While growing up in Louisiana, I used to be allowed the pleasure of extended visits to my grandparents. They, too, lived in Louisiana. Grandpa was a fun person to be around. We were real buddies and I enjoyed my visits with him very much. He would take me along when he went to town. That was something Dad didn't usually do. Grandpa found the time to take me fishing. He liked to point out things to me that I hadn't noticed. Seldom were we together that he didn't point out a 'coon, a possum, or an armadillo. Sometimes it was a bird I'd never seen before. Maybe he'd encourage me to listen to a particular bird's call. Always something.

"Grandpa always treated me real good—until ...

"Wait! I forgot to mention Grandpa's chickens and ducks. He had both. The ducks were domesticated, but they looked very similar to wild mallards. The chickens were white leghorns and good egg producers.

"Duck eggs are bigger than chicken hen eggs. But, Grandpa raised the tame ducks to eat, not so as to eat the eggs. Grandpa kept some drakes, that's what the males are called, so the eggs would be fertile. At all times, there seemed to be one or more of the ducks setting on from five to twelve eggs. It took about four weeks for them to hatch. The ducklings are ready and able to swim the day after they're born.

"Since there were a few roosters among the leghorns, the chicken eggs were fertile, too. And that's where the story comes in.

"I found a duck setting on a nest of only six eggs. The 'imp of mischief,' found in boys, talked me into putting six hens eggs in the nest. I did it. The duck never complained a bit.

"Almost to the day, four weeks later, the eggs all hatched. Sure enough, the next day, the duck took her brood of 'ducklings' to the pond. Half of them swam, half of them drowned.

"Grandpa found out and he was 'madder'n a wet hen.' It took quite a while before we were buddies again."

And, of course, his story reminded me of something that happened to me when I was a boy. A boy of nine, to be exact.

On the date of the particular experience it was late in the evening and Dad wasn't home yet. At this point in my life I hadn't yet learned to cook and I was hungry. "Where can I innocently bum a meal?" Well, I had never shown up at supper time at Cecil Christler's house and so I thought, "Why not?" Mrs. Christler's name was Grace, I think. One thing I do remember for sure about her was that she often wore men's clothing during the week. A hat, boots, overalls, and a lumber jacket. She worked hard, on the farm, right alongside Cecil. Mom said her attitude was, "If I'm going to work like a man, then I might as well dress like a man."

There was a problem. Just showing up at the door of Cecil Christler, I mean. The flock of geese! There were six geese and six ganders. I should say six pair, because they mate for life. I was more than a little afraid of the ganders.

Somewhere, I read, "The goose of the barnyard" first came from Europe. It is one of the proudest birds of the animal kingdom. The same article said, "Tame geese rank among the most intelligent of the many kinds of domesticated birds."

The ganders must have been smart because they knew I was afraid of them. They'd point their heads and run toward me, with their wings outspread and flapping, just as hard as they could. All the while, they'd be making a loud hissing sound. It was enough to scare the bejabbers out of any boy. This night was no different. They weren't in sight until I got almost to the kitchen door, then here they came. I just ran, as hard as I could, toward the road.

I stopped running as soon as they quit chasing me, and I felt the geese had deprived me of a meal. Somehow, they never came out onto the road. That must have been part of their "smarts." There they stood in the driveway, all six of them, with their heads held high.

Then, the boy "imp of mischief" took over. I picked a flat rock from the gravel road and let it fly. By the sheerest of accidents, I hit one of them! In the neck! His long, aristocratic, neck bent right at the spot where the rock hit him, and he started wildly running around in a circle.

I ran home, as hard as I could run.

My conscience bothered me something fierce.

The stone must have killed the gander I hit because, next time I went by, there were six geese and only five ganders.

Although I've felt bad about the incident all my life, I've never told anybody about what I did.

But, you want to know something? Those five ganders never chased and hissed at me again.

25

The Fruit Cellar

I'd never seen one like it before nor have I seen one like it since. Maybe some day I'll stop and see if it's still there.

I'm talking about the fruit cellar, of course. The one at the County Farm. You'd have had to see it to believe it.

Nobody ever told me who built the "house of many rooms," called the County Farm, or how long ago it was built. I do know there was a row of fairly good sized Maple trees on each side of the driveway leading from the road to the house. The size of the trees would indicate that it had been there for a good long time before I started visiting there in 1932. The trees and the lane were probably put there at the same time the house was built.

Before the Great Depression there wasn't much excuse for being poor so it seems this big, impressive, home was built for housing poor people. Still, who knows? Even the Bible says, "You have the poor always with you."

Over by Emma Lake was the Rodgers Orphans Home. No doubt some of the children there came from broken homes. Broken because of money problems. Not being able to support one's family has always carried a dreadful stigma. There are those who claim the Bible says, "If anyone doesn't work, neither let him eat." However, in fact, at 2nd Thessalonians 3:10 it says, "If anyone does not want to work, neither let him eat." Yes, there were numerous people who wanted to work but there were very few paying jobs to be had.

Many of the residents at the County Farm were elderly people who had lost their means of livelihood and even lost their homes. "Too old to start over again," as some would say. Other were infirm in some way or another and had to have special care. None were completely bedridden.

A few at the home were retarded and others described as "mental cases." Mostly they were harmless and never exhibited violent behavior. Commonly, they either wouldn't talk at all and viewed others with a good deal of suspicion, or they talked to an imaginary person constantly. In fact, they seemed to be carrying on a conversation.

The inmates of the County Farm, having mental problems, could seldom be counted on to do any kind of real work. On the other hand, they generally were able to bathe and dress themselves and take their meals with the others in the main dining hall. One thing for sure, there was no abuse of anybody staying at the County Farm. Austin Merriman would never have tolerated it.

The reason I've mentioned there being some women and some men at the County Farm that were physically able to work is the simple fact that they were allowed to work. Expected to work, in fact. And without pay. One thing they all helped with was the filling of the fruit cellar. There was no need for any coaxing or cajoling because everybody would benefit from a full fruit cellar.

Between the driveway, house, and yard of the County Farm and the Norris farm on the east, was a kind of shallow ravine. The fruit cellar was built into the west bank of this ravine. Only the door on the front was exposed. In fact, it was the only door. The floor was dirt and the walls were stone. The ceiling was made of logs. It never seemed to get wet but was always cool and dry. It could have been used as a storm cellar and I don't know that it wasn't.

I can't truthfully remember how big it actually was but it was so much larger than anything I had seen before that it looked huge to me. A king-sized garden had to be raised in order to have an adequate supply of fresh vegetables during the summer and fall. The garden also had to produce enough for winter meals. There was no cold storage or freezer so most vegetables were canned. There were English peas, green snap beans, tomatoes, tomato juice, beets for pickling, corn, and lots of it. They wound up in row upon row of two-quart jars, open kettle-canned.

Sauerkraut was put down in ten gallon earthenware crocks and tens of bushels of Irish potatoes were kept in this dry storage. Turnips, carrots and beets were kept there as long as possible, too.

Then, there were sacks, as well as crates, of acorn squash and pumpkins. A fun winter experience was shelling and popping the popcorn that was stored still on the cob. Pickles? There were two-quart jars of sweet chunk pickles and mustard pickles. Dill pickles were favored, so there were more of them than all the other kinds. Relishes, too.

Another convenient and welcome attribute of the County Farm was the fruit trees. This meant peaches and pears to can as well as apple sauce to make. Some of the pears were as hard as bullets. It was well into winter before they ripened but they made fresh fruit, at that time, anyway. The orchard supplied the farm with different kinds of apples and some of them lasted all winter. Fresh popped popcorn and a crisp apple! Who could ask for anything more?

Austin and Alice Merriman tried very hard to see that a good table was set for the residents of the farm. It was their desire to make everybody feel at home. It was the belief of this loving couple that each resident would be better able to maintain a certain dignity, under the circumstances, if they were allowed to "help out." For that reason, all who were able were encouraged and invited to help plant and keep up the gardens and then to pitch in when it was canning time.

The tranquillity that existed at the County Farm during the tenure of the Merrimans would indicate they had the right idea.

The fruit cellar? To my nine year old way of thinking, it represented "The Horn Of Plenty."

26

I Remember Dan Lobsiger

Dad was talking. "Dan's powerful and strong as a Jersey Bull and it's a good thing, too. That cultipacker would have crushed an average man to death."

I'd heard vague stories about Mr. Lobsiger's accident, but I didn't really know what happened. I just knew he had a real pronounced limp. The reason the subject came up was that we were pulling up in his driveway and he was walking toward us. He walked kind of like his one leg was three or four inches shorter than the other. Actually, that might have been exactly right.

We'd been at the Homer Shoup farm across the road and now we were stopping at Dan Lobsiger's. Dad was lining up sheep shearing jobs, or anything else that paid hard cash. We were really strapped.

Homer had a brother named Orlie and a son, Harley. They all worked long and hard to keep a productive as well as an attractive farm.

The Lobsiger's had a big yard both front, back, and alongside their house. The back and side yard were literally covered with different pieces of farm equipment. The center part of the long barn was covered, too. I discovered that when I was snooping—er—uh—exploring. I did that while Dad was talking to Mr. Lobsiger. After a little while I had some help from Dan's son, Herman, and his stepson, Kelly Wells. They both entertained me by showing me around the yard and through the barn. Mr. Lobsiger always kept them both busy most all the time and this gave them an excuse for taking some time off.

The cultipacker! That's what I had wanted to see.

"What happened? How did it happen? Whose fault was it that Mr. Lobsiger got run over by this cultipacker?" I was full of questions and couldn't hold them in.

"It was Herman's fault! He was suppose to be holding the horses," Kelly said.

"Wasn't either my fault! It was those western horses Pa bought. Those Mustangs weren't broke for farming and they still aren't. I'm not going to take the blame. Anyway, there's nothing we can do about it now." Herman didn't want to be held responsible and I could understand why. You see, his dad was always going to be lame the rest of his life because of the accident.

Back in 1932, a tractor was a comparatively expensive piece of machinery and few farmers could afford one. Because of the shortage of money, horses were expensive, also. But, western horses? Now, they were something different. Thousands upon thousands of horses were running wild in many of the western states. They weren't as big as most farm horses but they were fleet of foot and wild.

Western ranchers considered the herds of wild horses a menace in more ways than one. They'd not only eat grass the ranchers wanted for their cattle but the wild stallions would often lure the ranchers mares into the wild. It wasn't easy to get them back.

Ever so often, the ranchers would get all their cowboys together and they'd round up a big herd of these small wild horses called Mustangs. First off, they'd cut out any horses that were branded or were obviously not part of the wild bunch. These they'd keep, along with any others they especially liked the looks of. The rest they'd ship back east to sell. The prices were usually not a lot more than the shipping charges, but at least they'd be rid of them. And, that's how and why the Lobsiger's came to have four Mustangs.

The cultipacker was a heavy piece of farm machinery used to break up clods of hard dirt. These clods didn't usually form unless the field had been too wet when it was plowed. Big rocks were often tied on top of the cultipacker to make it even heavier. As I recall the story, Dan and Herman, were hitching all four of these Mustangs together to pull the cultipacker. It wasn't easy, but they finally got the job done. For some reason, Dan was standing between two of the horses and Herman was holding them. But,

95

they broke loose from him and started pulling forward! Dan fell to the ground between the horses and they pulled the cultipacker right over the top of him!

When Dan realized it was inevitable he was going to be run over, he turned on his side, braced every muscle in his body, and waited until it had passed completely over him.

Like Dad said, "If he were an average man, it would have broken every bone in his body." But, not Dan Lobsiger. He wasn't an average man.

Dr. Shrock closed up the cuts in his head and arm and put a splint on his broken leg. That was it. His broken ribs healed as did his other cuts and bruises. Only the broken leg gave him trouble later on and that would likely have healed better had he stayed off it like the doctor had told him to. But, no! He couldn't stand the thought of laying around doing nothing, so he was soon up and at 'em.

Also stored in the barn were two pieces of machinery that fascinated me. A threshing machine and the big steam engine tractor that gave it its power! I'd never seen this particular set but had always looked forward to the arrival of Ed Miller and his threshing rig. His tractor was the biggest I'd ever seen. I remember, too, his blowing the steam engine's whistle as he approached the house. The lug marks were visible in the road long after threshing was over or until it rained.

Ed Miller was an inventor of sorts. It's said, "Necessity is the mother of invention." Maybe there wasn't any real "necessity" to have a ten bottom plow, at that time, but Ed decided to rig one up. For one thing, he thought it a shame to have that big steam engine tractor and use it only at threshing time.

One use Mr. Miller found for the steam engine was furnishing the power for his buzz saw. But, what he really wanted was some help with the plowing. It was customary to pull a single bottom plow with two horses. He did all his farming with horses except threshing and that required this big tractor.

Here's what he did:

Along with his own, he borrowed enough single furrow plows to make ten.

Then he elaborately, or maybe simply, attached them to a long pole so he could pull all ten at one time. The engine pulled them easily enough but, somehow, he could never figure out a way to get this contraption to turn corners. The idea was good but way ahead of its time. Dan Lobsiger should have used his steam engine instead of the mustangs to pull his heavy cultipacker. That would have worked.

Threshing machines and single bottom plows are almost, but definitely not entirely, a thing of the past.

Every man owes it to his children to make some arrangement for them to see a threshing operation in action. It's to be found in any Amish community.

Until this happens, they'll never fully appreciate a loaf of bread.

27

Learning a New Baseball Rule

Shipshewana High School didn't have much of an enrollment compared to today's consolidated schools. The facilities left much to be desired. But the students had spirit and the teachers had ability and enthusiasm.

Riley Case was one of the finest teachers and administrators anybody could have asked for. Like many small town principals, Mr. Case was a hard worker for his school, a strong dispenser of encouragement. I remember his being at our farm talking to Dad. His aim was to make sure all the Woodworth boys went to High School.

Tom Sovine was the coach at "Shipshe." He was a big fellow and thought all boys should play basketball. And baseball. Considering the facilities they had to work in, Coach Sovine did a good job. The gymnasium was such a derelict building it was dubbed "The Sheepshed." They stored the school bus bodies on the gym floor during the summer months. While school was out, they mounted truck bodies on the chassis so there'd be no down time.

One of his basketball and baseball playing students was Vanus Miller. During the year we lived in the parsonage, Vanus married my sister Edie. Truman Oesch, also a Shipsewana High School graduate, had taken my sister Mary to be his bride an Jan. 1. 1930. Truman and Mary lived near the Topeka Roller Mills, where he worked.

Vanus and Truman played both basketball and baseball in High School. Both were very good. They may not have been best friends, at the time, but they became so after they married my sisters. Both enjoyed coming to our house on Sunday afternoon. There was no basketball but plenty of baseball. It was on one of those Sunday afternoon picnics and baseball sessions when I learned how the baseball rules are sometimes made up as you go along.

It was a nice warm summer day. Mom was home on this particular weekend so all my brothers and sisters had come for Sunday dinner. Vanus and Truman were there, too. There were others including Harry Hart and his family and I remember a man my brothers called "Sully."

For dinner Mom had fixed fried chicken with mashed potatoes and gravy. I suspect Mary might have brought the chicken. We'd emptied out the basement when we left the farm and had lots of canned goods, so Mom mixed a quart of tomatoes with a quart of corn and served it hot. All it had for seasoning was salt and pepper. For dessert my sister Edie had baked a three layer chocolate cake. Everyone had a slice of chocolate cake served with Mom's mouth watering cornstarch pudding. A feast fit for a king, I thought.

In the afternoon, we played baseball. Several incidents still cling to my memory and I'll try to recall as many as I can.

Vanus was the catcher and Sully was the pitcher. As Sully would wind up to pitch, Vanus would call out, "Fire it down through that old dark alley, Sully Ole Boy." Then after the pitch and the batter hadn't swung at it, Vanus would throw it back saying, "He couldn't even see it, Sully Ole Boy." Then it would start over.

One time, when Harry Hart was the batter, Harry took a mighty swing at the ball and connected with a grounder toward third. He dropped the bat and took off running for first base as hard as he could. It was no use! Lloyd had grabbed up the ball at third and fired it back to Truman, playing first base, before Harry could make it there.

"Yer out!" shouted Vanus who was umpire as well as catcher.

Harry wasn't really what you'd call a young man, so he was puffing pretty hard when he stopped running. As he started walking back in the direction of home plate, he said, "A good smash like that deserves to be rewarded by a chew of tobacco." Whereupon, Harry pulled out his pouch of Red Man and started stuffing one side of his mouth with it.

"Whatta you mean, reward? You didn't get a hit," Sully called out to him with friendly sarcasm.

"Son, in this life, you need to reward yourself at every opportunity. I put forth my best effort. I did as well as I could and that's deserving of a reward."

Harry had a point, although I didn't think a chew of Red Man was much of a reward.

The incident I wanted to tell about happened after everybody was pretty well tired out.

Wayne had been at bat and had gotten a hit. Trying to stretch a single into a double he found himself trapped between first and second base. Wayne was fleet of foot but so was Truman. Charles was playing second base and as Wayne ran back to first, Charles threw the ball over Wayne's head to Truman. Wayne wheeled and started back to second. Truman then threw the ball back to Charles.

It was about the second exchange, and when Wayne was running toward second, that Truman tossed the ball so it bounced off Wayne's back. Then, Truman caught it.

"You're out!" Truman shouted. "I touched you and you're out!"

Wayne had run past Charles and was standing on second base.

"What do you mean, I'm out? The ball might have touched me but you didn't have it in your hand." Wayne wasn't about to give up without an argument. Everybody was ready to quit and welcomed the diversion. All came and joined in the argument, taking sides.

And that's how I learned a new baseball rule.

"You're out if you can't prove the ball wasn't in the opposing players hand when it touched you."

A Truman Oesch rule.

28

Toddy Bontrager

Dad's philosophy used to be, "Don't start something you can't finish." Maybe, that's why he never started too many things. He was afraid he couldn't finish. The things he did tackle, however, always seemed to turn out top-notch. He could plow the straightest furrow I ever saw, and that's the truth. He always cut our hair and he did it painstakingly. It was always a perfect job but it didn't happen often enough. He could shoot a .22 rifle with unbelievable accuracy. Always found more mushrooms than the rest of us. 'Cept maybe Wayne.

Like most boys, we were proud of our father. A little disappointed sometimes, but always proud. One thing he did better than anybody else was shear sheep. I've heard many farmers talk about it. Maybe it wasn't much to talk about but we boys liked it when somebody praised our Dad's ability. I worked with Dad nearly every day during the spring, helping shear sheep.

The country schools were in session only eight months out of the year with four months summer vacation. However, there wasn't any spring break in late March or early April as there is now. Most of the sheep shearing was done in May or June, which was during vacation time, but numerous farmers wanted their shearing done in April. Since I was the manpower that turned the crank of the sheep shearing machine I missed a substantial amount of school.

During my first three years at school my teacher, Amos Hostetler, never once sent a note home to my parents. Not that I remember anyway. Miss Neely, my teacher at Saylor School, wrote several and they were mostly complaining because I hadn't brought a note from Dad explaining why I'd missed school the day before. It never fazed him one bit. "Just tell her I needed you to help me shear sheep." And that was it.

Working with Dad, I got to meet many more people than I would have otherwise. I remember a fair percentage of the farmers we sheared sheep for and at least some of the events surrounding the one day job. It was unusual, although it did happen, for a farmer to keep a flock of sheep big enough so that we couldn't shear all of them in one day.

Dad had a lot of trouble with his back and his legs. One leg in particular. When he was a young man he hurt himself playing football. The leg had swollen badly and the doctors didn't really know what to do. When they cut into his leg, exploratory surgery is what we'd call it now, they accidentally severed his sciatic nerve. He never fully recovered from the effects of that surgery. Most likely that's why shearing sheep was such a back breaking job for him.

Our working hours, or our starting times at least, were often erratic. A good deal depended on what Dad had done the day or night before. If everything went well we'd get an early start so we could stop at the DX station and buy some gas and some light weight oil for lubricating the clippers on the shearing machine. No matter how hard he tried to gauge his finances Dad never seemed to have enough money to completely fill the tank with gas.

Most all farmers are early risers. Usually, they're out in the barn doing the milking when the sun comes up. It's been my experience that the farm wife doesn't always get up at the same time but still manages to have breakfast ready when her husband comes in from milking.

It was Dad's intention to arrive after milking and breakfast was over. The farmer was then able to help us set up for shearing.

Dad was always embarrassed when some farm wife would ask me if I'd had breakfast and I'd have to be honest and say "No." Because of that, but not always, we'd stop in town to get something to eat. Now, that doesn't mean we'd stop at a restaurant for breakfast. More often than not it meant stopping at Billy Davis's or Ralph Terry's meat market.

In all the years of our growing up my siblings and I were never once treated to a restaurant meal by our father. Not once!

This particular morning was no different. After buying two gallons of gas for the Model T Ford and a quart of oil for the sheep shearing rig, we had pulled up in front of Ralph Terry's Market. After Dad checked his snap pocket book to make sure he had enough money, we went inside the market.

"Good morning, Cecil. I see You've got your helper with you today."

"Yes, I have, Ralph. And he's hungry, as usual. I declare! I believe the boy's possessed of a tape worm, he eats so much."

"He's just a growing boy, Cecil. It's normal for them to be hungry all the time. What are you gonna feed him this morning?"

Neither of them spoke directly to me. I wasn't encouraged to talk because children were supposed to be seen and not heard.

On the counter was a huge cake of dark yellow cheese. It had a cover over it that looked like isinglass. The cheese was a good foot and a half across and no less than six inches thick.

Mr. Terry saw me looking at it so he said, still without speaking directly to me. "Betcha'd like to sample that cheese." Without any further ado he took the lid off and, with his big old knife, sliced me off a pretty fair-sized sliver of cheese.

I said, "Thank you, Mr. Terry," and started eating. He just smiled and turned his attention to Dad. The cheese was mild and delicious. Tasted like what we now call Colby or Longhorn. Maybe, County Line. I just know that I liked it and Dad could tell by my reaction.

"All right, Cecil. What are you going to buy for this boy to eat? And yourself, of course?"

"Well, I'd wanted to get a bottle of milk for us to share and a ring of bologna. But the boy sure likes that cheese. I've only got a quarter, a nickel, and some pennies. We've been having it rough, you know." Dad was proud and he hated to admit just how hard up we were.

"Tell you what I'm gonna do, Cecil." I've since learned all salesmen use that term. "I'll let you have a quart of milk, a ring of bologna, and I'll slice you off about a half pound of that cheese, for that quarter. I won't even look if you and Ted help yourselves from the barrel of crackers over there."

"Sounds good to me and I'll take it." It was while we were standing alongside the meat counter, and next to the cracker barrel, that Toddy Bontrager came in. Dad had taken the skin off the bologna and given me about a third of the ring. He had cut the cheese in small cubes and we helped ourselves to it as it still lay on the counter. We passed the bottle of milk back and forth between us.

As Toddy came through the door, he said, "Heh-heh-heh-hello-Cece." Then he said, "Good morn-orn-orn-orn-orn-morning-Ral-Ral-Ral-uhuh Terry."

Both Dad and Mr. Terry said, "Good morning, Toddy."

I'd heard Dad talking to Mom about Toddy. Dad said he had springhalt which is a disease horses tend to get. It's also called stringhalt. Anyway, Toddy walked just like Dad had described. His legs were kind of stiff and he walked with a jerk. And he stuttered.

Pointing to the mound of freshly ground hamburger in the display case, Toddy said, "Gimme a cup-cup-cup- cup-couple of pounds of ham-ham-ham-ham-ham-hambur-hambur-hambur." Then suddenly, he pointed at the rings of bologna and said, without a trace of stutter, "Give me two rings of bologna."

Dad had just taken a drink of milk. He spewed it all over the meat display case. Both he and Mr. Terry laughed uncontrollably. Mr. Bontrager turned and stalked out of the store.

From this experience, I learned something about Dad's sense of humor. It wasn't always the same as mine.

I felt very sorry for Toddy Bontrager that morning.

29

Saylor School

Nobody had ever told me who the Saylor School was named after or who built it and when. It was a wood frame, one room, school with a lot of windows. Painted white, of course. Back in the 1920's and 30's it was a rarity to see a house or a school painted any color other than white. Unless, of course, it was brick and even then the trim was always white. Barns were red but houses were white. Tradition, no doubt.

There's no question about it, the school might have been wood frame but it was well built and had been well-taken care of. Though I don't know when it was built, I do know that at least four generations of the Slack family attended there.

The cemetery at the Bethel Church was known as the Saylor Cemetery. There must have been some connection but I don't know what it was. Next time I go visit I think I'll go inspect some gravestones and see if I can find the name "Saylor."

During the one year I attended Saylor School the teacher was Elizabeth Neely. Miss Neely, we called her. Out of her hearing, the bigger boys called her "Red Head." She truly did have red hair. And freckles. She had an iron jaw too, but she was a good teacher.

Some of the students names come back to me from time to time. There were a lot of Troyers and I can't remember them all. I do remember Sam and Glada and Goldie, but I'm positive there were others. Sam was a good friend of Don Presdorf. Don had a brother, Bob, and their father's name was William or Bill. I can still picture him.

There was June and Chuck Parsons and two members of the Slack family. Bruce and Hazel Slack were the fourth generation of Slacks to attend Saylor School. Then, Robert Eaton and Frank Olmstead's boy. The Olmsteads lived between our house and the school. Also, several Kerns children. Evelyn was in my class. Arthur was her left-handed, baseball-pitching brother. Jim and Chester Rigsby lived south of the school just a little way. And I couldn't ever forget the Shrock family that lived next door to me. Altogether, there must have been something over thirty students spanning the eight grades that attended there.

Miss Neely had her hands full, teaching all those different grades and each one with a variety of subjects, yet she always managed to have some time for some "one on one" when it was necessary. Children seem to learn more if they know a teacher is really interested in the progress of each student. Miss Neely didn't think I had any need of one on one with her because she knew my brother, Charles, would help me if she didn't. She did help me in spelling.

Spelling was something Miss Neely liked and I firmly believe she did a better job teaching it because she liked it. With her help, I became downright proficient at spelling and arithmetic. Fact is, I won the fourth grade spelling contest at Saylor school. I then won the township spell down and came in either third or fourth in the county. At the final spell down, I missed the word, "meant." Can you believe it? I spelled it "m-e-n-t."

Boy, was I embarrassed!

When I came back to school after having missed such an easy word, Miss Neely said, "You did well Ted, better than I thought you would."

Mom and Dad were both good spellers. Come to think of it, all my family were good spellers!

But, let me tell you about a special spelling bee!

In rural areas, the church was the gathering place for many functions. However, they were mainly attended by members of the church. When the whole community had a get together, it was held at the school house. This especially applied if it involved only the school children of a particular school and the parents.

I remember only one spelling bee at Saylor School, but it was special to me. The reason it was special was that my mother won. My mother won! Mine! Everybody in the boundary of Saylor School's territory was invited, even farmers whose children were out of school and those who didn't have any to begin with.

You know something? I don't remember my dad going to any school function except a spelling bee. He was there this time, too. Each family brought sandwiches or baked beans or potato salad. Or maybe a big pan of fried chicken. There was lots of food and I liked that. While we ate, the men folk told stories and laughed boisterously at every one of them. They were really "turned on." I can't remember Dad ever sounding happier.

I not only liked to hear my dad laugh, but I liked to see him laugh. He had nice looking teeth and one of his front teeth was gold. That looked mighty impressive to me considering how poor we were. A genuine gold tooth!

Well, anyway, we finally got down to the spelling bee. Everybody stood up around the outside of the room with Miss Neely in the center. She was the one who gave out the words. On the desk she had several spelling books that she was going to use. She didn't have any special list of spelling words.

The children were given words from the book that went with their class. The eighth graders and the parents got words from the eighth grade speller. When a word was misspelled, the one who had made the mistake had to take a seat and the next person in line got a chance to spell the word. If they missed, "down they went" and the next one tried. This went on until the word was spelled correctly. Naturally, the last one standing was the winner of the "spell down."

Most people tend to try to forget losing situations and I am no exception, but I always considered this contest a "winner." Although I had been eliminated earlier, along with brother Charles and Dad, Mom was still standing at the finish. She and William Presdorf.

Miss Neely said, Mr. Presdorf, spell "grammar."

Mr. Presdorf said, "Grammar. G-r-a-m-m-e-r. Grammar."

"Wrong" intoned Miss Neely. "Mrs. Woodworth, spell grammar."

As Mr. Presdorf sat down, Mom said, "Grammar. G-r-a-m-m-a-r. Grammar."

"That is correct and you are the winner!"

Everyone applauded vigorously and now it was time to go home.

I was very proud of my mother. She was a great lady.

P.S. In later years I found that an old time farmer named William Saylor was the donor of the land used for the Saylor School and Cemetery. Also, the school was built before 1874 and, in some records, was said to be on land owned by Josiah Eaton.

The Saylor School

30

Go Sit In The First Grade Row, Ted!

"It's all in you're attitude, Ted, and you have a bad attitude! We live here and that's a fact. You're going to go to Saylor School and that's a fact. You might as well get used to it because nothing is going to change."

Dad was lecturing me again because I'd complained about going to a new school and that Miss Neely, the teacher, didn't like me. At least, I didn't think she did.

Dad wasn't finished. Not anywhere near. Once he got started he was hard to stop. He settled in on a diatribe, as Mom used to call it, against all politicians and bankers. "They're all a bunch of highwaymen and robbers! If your grandfather were still alive he'd have found a way to save the farm and it'd have been 'a horse of a another color.' We'd still be living there and you'd be going to Green School, just like the last three years. All my children went there and so did my brothers and sisters and me. My mom, too."

Every time he went on and on like that, I felt sorry for him and forgot about my own problems. Maybe that's the way he had planned it, but I don't think so. Dad had always figured to inherit the farm we had lived on but it wasn't to be so. He was very bitter about how things had worked out and he blamed politicians and bankers, rather than his Pa, for the stock market crash and the resultant hard times. No work and no money. It was tough to make ends meet and most of the time we didn't.

"It would be easier for both of us if you'd just take things the way they are and do your best with what we have. Our situation is bound to get better. It's a lead cinch it can't get any worse."

Little did he know what the future had in store for us.

In fact, like so many people in those depression years, Dad had a negative as well as a defeatist attitude. It was as though the whole world had come tumbling down all around him and had tried to

109

land smack onto his shoulders. He seemed to have lost his drive. Each day was more difficult to face than the last, but he tried.

Dad used to say that everybody was a philosopher, but most people didn't practice their own philosophy. I guess it was kind of like the common remark, "Don't do as I do but do as I say." One of Dad's gems was, "You'll eventually reach any goal if you just keep putting one foot in front of the other." Sounds reasonable. Simple, but reasonable.

Often, Dad used to give me a ride to school in the morning. It was no trouble for him because it was only a mile and it was on his way to town. I never knew for sure what Dad found to do in town. He'd talk about it, sometimes. There were park benches in the Court House yard as well as some kind of a bench in front of most every store in town. He'd often just sit and reminisce about the "good ol' days" with his friends. Other times he'd play cards or shoot pool. More than once, he mentioned congregating with friends at Roy "Shorty" Rhodes Packard dealership and garage. "Just talking," he said.

Meanwhile, back at Saylor School, recess was always my favorite period.

There weren't enough of them. To me, study and homework were the bane of a school boy's life. It was years, and almost too late, before I became convinced that an education was a good thing to have. Now, of course, I regret not having tried harder.

At Saylor School, I just couldn't seem to get my brain shifted into a learning gear. It wasn't as though I had any kind of a learning disability, it was more like I wasn't properly motivated. At Green School I had tried very hard because I wanted to please my teacher, Amos Hostetler. He tried to make each of us feel good about ourselves. It was effective psychology that worked wonders.

There was another problem and it likely was the major one. Dad didn't pressure me very much to do my homework. Mom used to help me and so did my brothers and sisters. But, they were all gone.

Every teacher seems to have her own personal brand of punishment for misconduct or laziness. Miss Neely was no exception. While Mr. Hostetler tended to rule by threat of the tailor made paddle, Miss Neely used what could only be described as "cruel and inhuman punishment."

Let me tell you what she did.

Saylor School was a one room school where the first through the eighth grades were taught by only one teacher. Because of the disparity in size of the students, the school desks were of different sizes. The seats and desks were permanently mounted on long slats so the whole row of desks could be moved at the same time.

Miss Elizabeth Neely, our teacher

Now, the first grade row had much smaller seats than the eighth grade. As a matter of fact, there were at least four different sizes of seats. Well, anyway, another Monday morning came and arithmetic class finally arrived. I didn't have my homework finished, again. Miss Neely, a red head, lost her temper.

"Go sit in the first grade row, Ted!" she shouted. I was in the fourth grade. "If you're going to do first grade level work and act like a first grader, then you're going to sit in the first grade row!" She was really angry.

The back seat of the first grade row! How humiliating! I was nine years old and could hard squeeze myself into the first grade-sized seat. I'd never be able to hold my head up again.

Nearly without exception, the other students poked fun at me. Even my brother, Charles. His only comment was, "You brought it on yourself. Maybe now, you'll do your homework."

This punishment lasted for only a week, but you know, it's amazing how much smarter I became in just one week. I vowed never to let myself be put in that position again. Before the year was over, I excelled in arithmetic. Matter of fact, I wound up with the best grades in the fourth grade in arithmetic-and spelling. I represented Saylor School in the township spelling contest and won. Then, I placed third in the county contest. Motivation! That's what it takes. And both Amos Hostetler and Elizabeth Neely knew how to motivate me.

31

My First Black Eye—Almost!

Children do not like to change schools. I was no exception. After spending my first three years at Green School, it was very difficult to face switching to Saylor School for the fourth grade. I didn't know anybody there except my brother, Charles, who had been sent to live with the Merril Eaton family after we left the farm. Well, there was one other.

When we lived on the farm, we used to haul and spread gravel to keep the road, in front of our farm, in good repair. The gravel pit was on the farm belonging to Elmo Neely. We used to stop at his house, once in a while, and we also sheared his sheep in the spring. It was there I had met Elizabeth Neely, the teacher at Saylor School. She was Elmo Neely's daughter.

Miss Neely, as we called her, was red headed and had a fair complexion. She had freckles too, as I recall. I remember thinking Jack Dempsey could have hit her on the chin and she wouldn't have flinched. Her lower jaw looked as solid as pure steel. I was afraid of her the first day at school. When I got home from school that first day, I told Dad who the teacher was and how I felt about her. He said, "Ted, I've known Elizabeth since the day she was born. She's a fine lady and will make you a first class teacher, even though she isn't a man."

I was surprised at his attitude because he'd always made it a point to say that only men were qualified to be country school teachers. "No job for an old maid," he'd say.

Dad continued, "If she's half as smart as old Elmo Neely, she'll make you a good teacher and that's for certain. Elmo Neely's the only farmer in these parts-well, almost the only one-with a substantial amount of money. 'Honest' money, that is. He might not have worked any harder than the rest of us, but he worked a "good deal" smarter than most of us. I don't begrudge him one bit. And Elizabeth has a firm set to her jaw, that's all. She's definitely not an old maid, either. Probably not more than 22 or 23 years old. Fact of the matter is, I'm 'pleasured' she's going to be your teacher."

It occurred to me that he was saying nice things about Miss Neely because there wasn't any choice. She was going to be my teacher whether I liked it or not.

As it turned out, I learned to like her very much. The set of her jaw was actually "resoluteness" or maybe, "determination." She could look very stern when the situation called for it. She could look awfully attractive too, when she smiled. One of the times we would get to see her smile, and show her pretty, white teeth, was when Clare McCally would stop by the school house at noon recess. The girls said she was "sweet" on him. They must have been right because, later, she married him and they had three children. One daughter and two sons.

It would be nice if I could truthfully say that I never got in any skirmishes, or caused any trouble, while I attended Saylor School. But, I can't.

Let me tell you about an instance where I caused trouble.

Two of my school mates were Thelma and Bruce Slack. Thelma was a year older than me and was in the fifth grade. Bruce was enough younger that he was in the third grade. They shouldn't really have been attending Saylor because they didn't even live in the same township. But their Dad, Harley Slack, wanted them to.

Here is the reason why.

Away back in the mid 1800's, Bruce's Great-Great-Grandfather, Isaac Slack, bought the farm presently owned by Carl Dintaman. He lived there until Bruce's great-grandfather, William Slack, took over. In turn, Bruce's Grandfather, Charles, and then his dad, Harley, lived there. They all attended Saylor School and Harley wanted his children to go to his "Alma Mater" and so they did. Tradition! You know?

Most of the time, their dad brought Thelma and Bruce to school in the morning and picked them up again at night.

In cold weather, Mr. Slack used to wear a horse hair overcoat. He was a great big man-and tall. He looked almost as big as a horse and even more so with that coat on, for it was bulky. Bruce told me how his dad happened to have this unusual coat. Harley Slack's aunt had a beautiful buggy horse that "up and died." She engaged Harley to bury her beloved horse.

But, what did Harley do before he pushed the horse over into the big hole he'd dug? He skinned it! And, why not? It was dead!

Anyway, Harley took the hide to a tanning and leather shop in Three Rivers and they dried it and tanned it and what all it is they had to do so the hide could be used to cover a couch or-in this case-make a coat. He then took it to a tailor who made him a fine, expensive, not to mention absolutely beautiful, horse hair overcoat. It kept him nice and warm in the coldest weather. If he hadn't been such a big man, it might have made him tired just to have carried it around. You see, it weighed "nigh unto" fifteen pounds.

Back to the school yard.

During recess, a game was being played where all the players were to stand in a big circle, facing the center. There were two or three players on the inside of the circle. The name of the game was probably 'in jail' or something like that. The object was for those inside to try to push their way out. If they were able to get out, the weak link in the chain had to go inside the circle and take their place. The one who had been 'in jail' now became part of the chain.

Not all the students played and I was one who didn't. I just watched. Another was a new student, Jim Rigsby, who had recently moved to the neighborhood from Kentucky. He and his brother, Chester, lived with their grandmother.

Bruce Slack was part of the chain and watching those who were "prisoners" to make sure none of them pushed their way out. For no good reason I can think of, I pushed Bruce into the inside of the circle. I quickly stepped away from the spot where I had been standing. When Bruce regained his balance and ran back to his place in the circle, Jim was standing there. Bruce said, "Jim, you do that again and I'll give you a big black eye!"

Jim said, "I never touched you."

A little while later, I pushed Bruce again. Chester was standing beside me. I quickly moved a few steps back and looked innocent.

When Bruce regained his balance, he charged at Jim with both fists flying.

"I warned you and now you're going to get it!" Bruce yelled.

Miss Neely heard the commotion and rushed out to break up the fight. She broke it up, all right, but not before Jim Rigsby had gotten a big black eye that should have been mine.

After Miss Neely had considered all the accusations and excuses, she punished Jim and me. Bruce got off, scot free!

And the horse hair coat? Harley Slack still had it when he died at 99 years of age. Bruce has it now and he's even bigger than his father had been.

Harley Slack and his horse-hair coat

32

The County Commissioner

Less than a mile west of the George Dintaman farm was the home of Frank and Hazel McCally and their son, Clair.

The McCally's were married before my folks were and I know that because, somehow, I came into possession of a picture post card sent by my Dad to my mother. There's no doubt he sent the card during their courtship because he addressed it to Miss Sylvia Todd, LaGrange, Ind. Nothing more. Only "LaGrange, Ind."

Forming my opinion just on the message he sent, I would say, based on a scale of one to ten, Dad would have scored no more than a two in the romance department. The message was:

"We are invited to a party tonight at the McCallys. Will be down about seven and you can suit yourself about going. Cecil."

No salutation! No, "Dear Sylvia." No anything! Plainly, "We are invited . . ."

Then, he signed it simply, "Cecil." No, "Love, Cecil." Nothing. Just, "Cecil."

Another thing, he must have mailed it the same day as the party because he said, "We are invited to a party tonight . . ." In spite of practically no address, the postal service must have been much faster in those days than it is today.

The card was mailed with a one cent stamp bearing a picture of Benjamin Franklin on it. Oh, yes! The card was made in Germany. In the upper left hand corner on the side containing the address and message is the word "Post Card" in 17 different languages. Post Karte-Carte Postale - Brekfort-Correspondenzkarte-Unione Postale Universale-Cartao Postal and in Russian to name a few.

And the picture? Dad would have scored ten in the romance department if you were to base your opinion on the picture alone.

The card shows this young couple sitting on a log, facing in opposite directions. She has her hand on his shoulder and he has his arm around her waist. They're looking into each others eyes. The log appears to be laying in a bed of wild flowers. Near by is a rail fence, beyond which are green trees. Alongside the grove of trees is a white cottage which seems nestled in a valley. In the background is a mountain or a very high hill.

It is possible the two had been taking a walk or, perhaps, they'd just enjoyed a picnic together. Whatever the couple had been doing, it had been done in propriety. He was wearing a dark striped suit and she a long dark dress. In other words, they are attired in the "Sunday go to meetin'" clothes that were in style in 1900 to 1910. And that would most likely have been what Mom and Dad would have worn to the McCally's party.

The point is, my parents and the McCallys were good friends and, because of that, they must have known of my father's affliction. Speaking of my father's affliction, I remember the attitude of some people as being disdainful. Some considered him to be a lazy "ne'er do well." They didn't realize how he suffered from a botched operation at a reputable hospital. It's a long story. There's an old Indian proverb that fit his situation well.

It goes something like this:

"Never judge another Indian until you've walked a mile in his moccasins." Anyway, during the year my mother worked at the County Infirmary and Dad and I lived in the parsonage of the Bethel Church, Frank McCally was the County Commissioner representing Clay Township.

Since it was only a mile from the parsonage to the Saylor school, I always walked even in the winter time. I didn't see anything wrong with that, especially since I was in the fourth grade and had always walked to school. But, I want to tell you about one particular morning.

The weather had been relatively mild for that time of winter. Temperatures had been in the mid 40's, until this one night when there was this cooling trend and atmospheric conditions were just right to produce snow. Lots of it. Over a foot of damp snow. You know-the kind that packs into good, firm, snowballs.

From the kitchen window it looked really cold, what with everything being covered by snow. Even the trees. Since the snow was so wet it clung to the tree limbs making them look like "snow trees."

Dad was still in bed, so, bundling up good and warm. I headed out. I soon discovered it wasn't very cold and that the Shrock kids were already on their way to school ahead of me. Almost at once I realized the snow would pack well and pack it I did. Throwing at the trees along the road, most of the snowballs would stick wherever they hit. Walking to school was going to be fun, or so I thought.

Frank McCally came along and picked me up. Well, he didn't exactly pick me up. You see, I had already managed to get myself pretty well covered with snow and he wouldn't let me ride in the car. He made me ride on the running board. On the driver's side. He rolled the window down in order for me to hold on and so he could talk to me. Question me, actually. Hazel was with him and she leaned over in order to hear my answers to his questions.

Their car was a big, black, four door Dodge, as I recall. The steering wheel looked real big and I'm almost certain it was made of wood. For sure, the car had big disc wheels and they were covered with snow.

Mr. McCally watched me more than he watched the road. "Has Cecil been able to find any kind of work, Teddy?"

"No, not for a while." I answered.

"How does he buy food for the two of you?"

"Mom usually brings something for us when she comes home every two weeks." His questioning was making me very uncomfortable and I was wishing he hadn't come along. His driving scared me, too.

"You mean she brings home food from the County Farm?" He was just on the verge of shouting. I knew what he was implying.

"No, I don't mean that. She and Dad buy groceries when he picks her up and brings her home. That's what I meant."

He was still upset and watching me instead of the road. And then it happened.

"Frank! You're running off the road!" Hazel was shouting.

He was running into a ditch, and on my side, yet in the bargain. I jumped and just in time! When the car came to a stop, the running board where I had been standing was buried in the snow. The car was very nearly lying on its side.

All four wheels were still on the ground, although the left wheels were well buried in the ditch and the whole car tilted precariously.

Mrs. McCally was pushing the car door open on the passengers side. "Teddy! Teddy! Where are you? Are you all right?" She was really worried. She hadn't seen me jump just before Mr. McCally drove completely off the road.

"I'm all right, Mrs. McCally." I was almost buried in snow but I wasn't hurt. Had I waited another second or two before I jumped, I'd have been squashed by the big car.

Mr. McCally wasn't hurt either. Well, maybe his pride, a little. Hurrying on toward school, I stopped at Merril Eaton's and told them what had happened. Mr. Eaton, I later heard, hitched up his team and pulled the car out. Horses to the rescue, again.

That was one day I was glad, even happy, to get to school.

Cecil's postcard to Sylvia

33

George Dintaman, Psychologist and Farmer

My brother, Lloyd, counted Carl Dintaman among his best friends. If Carl had any brother or sisters, I never knew them and I don't seem to have a very clear remembrance of his mother, either. She must have been a meticulous housekeeper because her house was always "spic and span." For good reason, Lloyd thought a lot of Carl's dad, George Dintaman. Lloyd was able to draw on the psychology lessons George taught him in successfully raising five children of his own.

The Dintaman home was one of the several farms where Lloyd spent a good deal of his time while he was going to Shipshewana High School. George especially liked to have him there during summer vacation. I don't recall his ever having a hired man, but a couple of teenage boys, with the right supervision, can get a considerable amount of farm work done. And in this case, at little cost.

The Dintaman farm had been owned, back in the 1800's, by the Slack family. First was Isaac Slack, who built the two story frame house. Then his son, William, took over the operation of the farm as well as occupancy of the house. After that came William's son, Charles, who raised his family there. One of his sons was Harley Slack who married a daughter of Davis Gottschalk, across the road from Cecil "Toby" Christler. Their children were Thelma and Bruce Slack, neither of which took up farming. Now that I've got those statistics out of the way I can get back to the psychology of George Dintaman.

George was a subscriber to the theory that "Success is a journey, not a destination." He indoctrinated his son, Carl, with the same philosophy. In order to have a nice looking and productive farm you have to work at it constantly. Anybody who drives by the Dintaman farm today can appreciate that a nice looking farm requires constant care and attention. "Nothing ever gets done by itself."

One picture is said to be worth a thousand words. Bruce Slack furnished me an early photograph of the house on the Slack farm as it appeared in 1877 and a much more recent picture of what the Dintarnan farm looks like today. It's an interesting contrast.

George was a proud man. He tried to avoid doing things that would bring shame to bear on him or his family. If for no other reason, that should have made him feel proud. He used this "proud" thing as a tool for betterment. For example, "If you own a farm animal of which you are not proud, get rid of it! Like, you couldn't be very proud of a skinny, old, mangy dog. How about a bony, swaybacked, old horse with the heaves?" George wouldn't have had anything like that around because he wouldn't have been proud of it.

A dirty car? Never! And his farm buildings? They seemed always to be freshly painted, the lawn mowed and the hedges and trees trimmed. He was justly proud of all these things. The farm machinery was maintained in tip top condition and the fences never seemed to need mending. His whole farming operation was an exercise in preventive maintenance. He never let anything get completely broken down before he fixed it. Nor was anything allowed to become completely weather beaten before it was given a fresh coat of paint.

And that was the environment in which my brother Lloyd, developed some of his early working habits. It was definitely a "work ethic" that he learned by example from George Dintaman. Another part of his psychology was to convince the boys that they were having fun when they were working together and they enjoyed each others company. All work is easier when your working with friends.

One of the suggestions George made, and the boys followed, was to keep track of how many squirts of milk it took to fill a bucket. Counting soon became a fun thing. While shocking oats or wheat, they counted how many bundles it took to make a shock. At threshing time they counted how many bundles it took to fill a wagon. Then, counted them again when they fed the bundles into the separator. At haying time they counted how many forkfuls it took to fill the wagon. Counting. Always counting.

Yet another facet of George Dintaman's psychology was the technique of "compliments." Compliments on a job well done or having finished an assigned project, say, before milking time.

"Just look at what a neat job you boys did! No two boys I know could have done it any better! I'm proud of you."

He heaped praise on them and it was balm to their ears. It had the desired effect. They worked harder and enjoyed it more.

Lloyd profited from George Dintaman's psychology in that he always enjoyed working and never worked at anything he didn't enjoy.

Lloyd always tried to keep from getting involved in any work that tended to be extremely complicated. He ascribed to the KISMIF principle.

"Keep it simple. Make it fun."

The Isaac Slack Homestead as it is today

34

William Sherman Kerns, Sr.
Father of Fifteen

Wm. Kerns and his wife, the former Grace Peck, were plain old American Methodists. Their ancestry was partly German, partly American Indian, and partly-you name it. They were LaGrange county residents from away back. Their first child, Elmer, was born in 1900 and their last child, Herbert, was born in 1929. Meanwhile, they parented thirteen more for a total of fifteen. Six boys and nine girls.

It's possible that William was influenced by the Bible scripture at Genesis 1:28 where it says, "God blessed them and God said to them: 'Be fruitful and become many and fill the earth and subdue it. . . .'"

No matter what his reason, he and Grace were prolific to say the least. Their progeny are now uncountable.

William never felt an education beyond learning to farm was at all necessary. To him, "subdue the earth" meant to farm it. That attitude just very well might have contributed to the difference of opinion that culminated in the oldest son, Elmer, leaving home in mid-High School. They had a major falling out over something.

Elmer was befriended by a lawyer and his wife who evidently saw potential in him that William didn't or wouldn't. He lived with them until his graduation from LaGrange High School.

The lawyer must have had some good connections and Elmer some outstanding scholastic ability because Elmer attended, and graduated from, the United States Military Academy at West Point, New York. After graduation he spent 25 years in the Army and 12 years in the Air Force. A book could be written about his experiences in World War I, World War 11, and the Korean War.

Then there was Willmer Clinton, born in 1902. He prefers to be known as Clinton and still lives on the old Kerns farm north of LaGrange.

Next came Edith in 1903, Thelma in 1905, and Pauline in 1907. Pauline married tall, gangly, Lester Lacy Betts. I remember him well.

He worked for the Lumber Company and, of an evening, you'd find him at the Cigar Store playing cards. Rum, most likely. On weekends, he'd often take his sons fishing. Quality time, no two ways about it.

Given the opportunity and the desire, I suspect Lester could have become a successful pianist. The reason I say that is he had the longest fingers of any man I've ever seen. In addition, he kept his finger nails longer than the average person. They came in handy. You see, Lester rolled his own cigarettes from either Bull Durham or Dukes Mixture. He'd smoke the cigarette so short and close to his mouth that he'd have burned his fingers taking it out of his mouth. So, he took it out with his finger nails. Lester used to stutter when he was nervous and he'd get that way when anybody asked him his name. He'd always say "I'm Leh-Leh-Leh-Lester L-L-L-Lacy Beh-Beh-Beh-Betts." He was a nice man.

And then came Iona in 1909 and Helen in 191 1. Helen married Bill Foltz, the oldest son of our neighbors, the Reuben Foltz's.

Leola was born in 1913 and Clela in 1915. Clela married Marion Atwater who attended Green School along with my brothers and me.

Therman was next in 1917 and Arthur in 1919. They went into the Army together and served in World War II.

Arthur is the one that I remember best. Or worst. I'm not sure which. You see, when I attended Green School and we'd play baseball against Saylor School, Arthur was the pitcher. Of course, when I went to Saylor we were on the same team and I was glad of it.

I didn't mention that Art, as we called him, was left handed. His pitch was absolutely fierce! I was scared half to death when I came up to bat against him. It just didn't seem natural to see someone throw the ball so hard and do it with his left hand.

Next came Evelyn in 1922. She and I were in the same grade at Saylor School.

Marcella was born in 1924. My memory says she was above average in good looks and she had freckles. I could be wrong.

Finally, in 1927, they named a boy Junior. William Sherman Kerns Jr.

Last, but not least, Herbert was born in 1929. Herbert loves to fish. With or without ice. He and his wife, Helen, still live in Clay township. Out in the country, surrounded by farms.

William Kerns Sr. didn't have his way with his first son as far as education was concerned, but he did with the other fourteen. None of them ever attended college and, as a matter of fact, none of them completed four years of High School.

All fifteen of the Kern children lived through the Great Depression and that was an education in itself. "The College of Hard Knocks," they used to call it. Not a great amount of formal education but a bountiful amount of practical education.

It has been said that getting an education is just a matter of learning to get along with people. They all learned to do that, so, I'd say they all wound up with a good education.

Wouldn't you agree?

The William Sherman Kerns, Sr. family, 1968
Back Row: Art, Elmer, Herbert, Willie
Center Row: Pauline, Thelma, Clinton, Clela, Helen, Therman
Front Row: Edith, Leola, Iona, Marcella, Evelyn

35

The Todd Family Reunion

"LaGrange Couple, both 94, to observe 75th Wedding Anniversary Sunday" was the caption over a story in the South Bend Tribune in November of 1963.

They were talking about my Grandparents, Joseph and Edith Todd, of LaGrange, Indiana. Grandpa said, "Seventy-five years is a long time to be married to the same woman."

Zena and I celebrated our fifty years of married life last year, so we're two thirds of the way there. We'll make it, I promise!

Some of my fondest memories involve family reunions held yearly at Grandpa and Grandma Todd's farm home. Most of their descendants attended every year and it was the only time many of us saw each other until the next year. Dad was known to express the opinion that once a year was often enough. He always enjoyed himself, though.

Grandpa's sisters often used to attend, also. Great-aunt Opal Whitford came from Kendallville and two others came from California. One was Aunt Mattie. One or more of his nephews usually made it there. I remember "Cash" Todd from Toledo, Ohio and Frank Todd from White Pigeon. I don't think they were brothers. Uncle Ivan and Aunt Mildred Hill came from Harvey, and then from Pana, Illinois, when they moved there.

Grandma's half brother, Jay Conrad, his wife Pearl, and their son, Marion, used to attend sometimes. And there was Stanley Hackett and his dad from Vicksburg, Michigan.

Mostly, the adults or older folks sat around and talked about days long gone. I wish now I'd have listened to them. I did some, but not enough. We kids spent our time playing and running.

The cousins nearest me in age were Arnold Connelly and Janette Todd. Jack and Warren Todd were close enough that the five of us were together most of the time.

Uncle Henry Todd was always there with Aunt Eva and their children, Leora, Ruth, Warren and Janette.

Aunt Eva and Uncle Floyd Connelly always brought their boys Harold and Arnold.

Uncle Lewis Todd and Aunt Marie, with Robert, Keith, and Jack, always came. They only lived a mile away. Uncle Lewis used to drive a big, black, Dodge touring car that I considered to be definitely first class. Nothing is perfect and I remember the shiny, black, leather upholstery was blisteringly hot on our back sides in the summer time and bitter cold in the winter. There never seemed to be any in between.

All of the relatives from out of state were rich. Or, so we thought. How could you have the name "Cash" Todd and not be rich? He'd always drive all the way from Toledo, Ohio, which I thought was a very long ways. Cash smoked cigars and he always tilted his head to the side when he talked. He told of this magnificent and successful night club that he owned back home in Ohio.

One time, after a lot of discussion, Uncle Lewis and my cousin, Keith, took off for Ohio to verify or put the lie to Cash's bragging.

Following the directions they'd been given, it wasn't that hard to find the address, once they got to Toledo. In front of the store building was a rather plain sign that said, simply, TAVERN.

Keith said, "This can't be it. He said it was a big night club. This looks like nothing but a beer joint to me."

"You're going to find that Cash is more of a braggart than a successful business man." Uncle Lewis knew him better than Keith did.

Cash welcomed them with open arms. He wasn't the least bit embarrassed. To him his saloon was a magnificent and glamorous night club and not just a neighborhood bar.

"Beauty is in the eye of the beholder," it has been said.

And then there was Frank Todd from White Pigeon, Michigan. There could be no doubt he was wealthy. A number of relatives had seen the sign on his business establishment. "Todd Jewelers." All jewelers are rich, aren't they?

Nobody seemed to know a whole lot about the Hacketts from Vicksburg except that they always drove a nice car. Stanley usually had two girl friends with him. Dad always said, "That'll get him in trouble, some day." Uncle Henry Todd and Uncle Jay Conrad were partners, at one time, in the business of painting. They were the first ones in LaGrange county to own a paint spraying machine. It was definitely something new. Grandpa thought it was a newfangled contraption that would never take the place of hand held paint brushes.

Reunions have always been one of my favorite "things." Especially dinner, which was served at about one o'clock. The ladies used to try to outdo each other, so there was an abundance of food. Each had a specialty and brought plenty of it. Most all brought wicker baskets full of goodies.

Those were hard times, but a really good cook could do wonders with elbow macaroni mixed with any of several home-canned vegetables. You could count on there being several pans of fried chicken, and it wasn't deep fried in grease, either. Delicious! Pies? I think every household brought at least one pie. There was apple, raspberry, gooseberry, cherry, rhubarb and on and on. I'm gaining weight just thinking about it!

Janette and I used to pair off and eat dinner together. The other cousins poked fun at us, but we didn't care. We liked each other.

After dinner, a business meeting was held. The meeting primarily consisted of electing officers for the following year. Each year an effort was made to get Grandpa to be President for the following year. Starting at about the age 60, he came up with, "My back has been giving me a considerable amount of trouble this past year and I just might not be around next year. Give it to one of the younger ones. Give it to Ivan. He's good at that sort of stuff. He's the only one in the family with a half way decent education."

Have you ever seen a cherry bomb? They've been around for a long time. About the size of a big marble, these fire crackers will explode with a tremendous BANG when you throw one against cement or anything hard. Grandpa's house had a full basement. The walls of the basement were rock and cement. It extended up about two feet above the ground and the house stood on top of that.

One Saturday, before reunion Sunday, Jack bought four of these little bombs. They cost a penny each. I know he bought them because I never had any money. On Sunday he gave me two of them.

When Grandpa was nominated to be President for the next year, he stood up, rubbed his back, and said, "My back's been bothering me . . . ."

At that instant Jack and I threw both our cherry bombs at the cement wall.

They all hit at the same time.

"BOOM!"

You never heard such a racket in your whole life!

Everybody jumped about a foot-especially Grandpa. When everyone had settled down, Grandpa started to laugh. "If I can jump that high now, I just might be around here next year." With that he was elected President. Grandpa was around a bunch more years. He lived to the ripe age of 101 years.

I've always felt guilty about the cherry bomb incident. Somebody could have died of a heart attack.

Kids do some really dumb things!

Grandma Edith & Grandpa Joseph Todd at their 75th Wedding Anniversary

36

Mama's Cat, Named Ed, & Other Cats I've Known

My mother always had at least one cat. The cats on our farm must have numbered at least six. Only one was designated as Mama's cat.

There, I did it! I called her Mama! Now, why haven't I been doing that since I wrote my first story? That's what we called her when we were young and I think my sisters, Mary and Edie, called her Mama 'til the day she died.

I hadn't intended, at this time, to talk about what my siblings and I had called our mother. You've no doubt noticed that I get side tracked from time to time. But, while I'm on the subject, after several years of calling her Mama, we switched to Mom. Then, when we all started having children, Mom informed us she didn't want anybody calling her "Grandma." "As long as my folks are still living you call them Grandma and Grandpa. You can call me Ma and your Papa, Pa." Mama thought she looked too young to be a grandmother. So, her children and her grandchildren called her "Ma."

Since I've mentioned Papa, I might as well tell you that we always called him Papa, when we were young. I can't really explain why I've always referred to him as Dad in my stories. In later years we mostly called him Dad but in between Papa and Dad we called him "Pa." Clear as mud, right?

And, on with the cat story.

We all learned to like cats while we lived on the farm and then most of us have had at least one cat about all of our lives.

Wayne, especially, liked cats. But then, he understood cat language and was able to interpret for the rest of us. Our cats were either red tabby or silver tabby. And, of course, a mixture of the two. We referred to them as tiger cats, too.

Oh! Wayne? Talking for the cats? I was going to get around to that. Especially at milking time, the cats did a lot of talking. To the rest of us it sounded as though they were merely meowing, as cats will do. Not to Wayne. He understood them.

Mama's cat, Ed, was a big, red tabby, tom cat. He was the boss cat and gave most of the orders for the rest of the cats.

"Kame-lar, Tin we hass sum millich?" That's what Ed was saying, Wayne told us.

If Wayne was understanding him correctly, I think Ed must have spoken a little bit of Pennsylvania Deutsch, too.

Wayne said the cats, with Ed as their spokesman or spokes cat, had a name for each of us.

Sister Edie was the eldest young'un in our family and her name, according to Wayne, was "Keedy-blar." Next was sister Mary, and was "Canary Canute." Lloyd was supposed to answer to "Koy-blar" and Charles was "Chab-lar." Wayne said his name was "Kame-lar" and I was to answer to "Keb-lar."

They liked Wayne best because, when they asked for milk, he'd spray a stream of milk in their direction. They were all expert at following a stream of milk. Never seemed to miss a drop.

When we moved away from the farm Mama brought Ed with her. I was glad she did because, as it turned out, the church and the parsonage were both quite heavily populated with mice. Ed soon had them under control. Then he started expanding his domain in to the adjoining fields. Ed would kill field mice, moles, grasshoppers, birds—just about anything that came his way. He was a good hunter. Entertaining, too. I watched him many times as he would seem to almost bury himself in the grass as he slinked along preparing to pounce on an unsuspecting sparrow.

Ed was something of an embarrassment. It wasn't his fault. Mama shouldn't have named him Ed. One of our closest neighbors, on the farm, had been Ed Miller. Now, at the parsonage, our nearest neighbor was Ed Shrock. Both Eds laughed about the Cat's name but I don't think either of them really thought it was all that funny.

Wayne and Florence had a white cat they named Pokey. He was constantly on the prowl in Wayne's three acre truck patch. I think he likely saved a lot of the sweet corn crop from marauding squirrels and birds—and even rabbits.

My sister Edie is the one who gets carried away with cats. Ever since her husband, Vanus, died, she's had more than one cat. They keep her company, she says. They're mostly calico or tabby cats. Each of them has a name but she mostly calls them "you guys." Like, "Get down off that table! What am I gonna' do with you guys?" She loves them all. Her house has almost as many pictures of cats as it has grandchildren.

Ma's last cat was a white longhair called Pixy. When Mom died, Lloyd and Helen kind of inherited Pixy and she lived to be 17 years old. There's a story to how Ma and Pa came by the white cat they chose to name Pixy.

The folks had a big black tom cat that they called Tom. He was seldom allowed inside the house so he slept and ate on the back porch. One morning, after Tom had been out it "cattin' around" most of the night, Mom discovered he had brought home a friend. It was a white longhair kitten about three or four months old.

Dad figured it out right away. The beautiful white kitten was a female.

"Old Tom's decided to get married and settle down."

"But, the kitten's only about half grown." Mom said.

"So? Maybe he figgers to adopt her and as she grows up he'll train her the way he wants her to be. Then, when she's old enough, they'll get married. Some men would like to be able to do that."

They were both laughing. Mom said, sounding a little exasperated, "You men are all alike."

The kitten was soon named Pixy because of her mischievous nature. Mom said she was Pixyish.

Pixy never had any kittens by Tom or any other cat because Lloyd had her spayed.

Back to Mama's cat named Ed.

When we moved to the parsonage Mom went to work at the County Farm. On her first weekend home she discovered we had been keeping her cat in the basement at night. She was far from happy and wouldn't listen to us when we tried to explain.

"Poor Ed will get arthritis sleeping in that damp cellar!"

It wasn't really damp in the basement but we never kept Ed there any more. Mom had a thing about arthritis and she enjoyed reciting a poem she'd clipped out of a magazine.

It goes like this:

Arthritis

Arthritis is a dread disease.
It gets you in the wrists and knees,
It gets you in the neck and fingers,
And where it gets you there it lingers.
Arthritis pains at many points,
But most settles in the joints.
I rather doubt it ever goes
Into such regions as the nose,
Or eyes or lips or even ears,
For which let's offer three small cheers.

37

The Squirting Lapel Flower

Back in 1932 the town of LaGrange had hitching racks along three sides of the Town Square. Had them down some of the side streets, too. The racks next to the bank figure into my story.

The Town Square would more properly be called the Court House Square because the only building on the square was the Court House. Well, there was a gazebo where the band sat during band concerts each Wednesday night during the summer months. Then on each corner facing the main street was an artillery piece from WW I.

We kids used to sit on one of the guns and turn the crank that raised or lowered the long barrel. We knew we could play with it as long as we left the barrel in the raised position. Looked more menacing that way, I guess. There was also a big cannon in the square. Alongside was a pyramid of cannon balls. We used to ride the cannon and pretend it was a horse we were riding bareback.

Seems to me as though all those old relics of WW I were melted down to be used again in WW II.

On one corner of the square was a drinking fountain that ran perpetually. The fountain was made of cast iron and one drank water from little holes in a ball about the size of a big orange. There was a bowl around the top where the young ones could hold on with their hands while standing on another bowl closer to the ground. The bottom one held water for the dogs to drink. I think every dog in the town knew about the canine watering fountain. Dogs were seldom tied up and, as I recall, did a lot of roaming.

At mention of the drinking fountain I feel somehow compelled to repeat a story told to me last year by Bob Waddell. Admittedly, he told me a number of stories but, at this time, I only want to tell this particular one because the drinking fountain is involved.

Bob said to me, "I've never had the nerve to write this story or even tell it to very many of my friends. You might even want to wait until the time is right before you tell it." I've decided this is the right time.

The Sheperdson Abstract Office was in the middle of the block across from the Court House. The business was operated by Pearl Will and her daughter, Mary Jane. Due to their many transactions with the County Clerk, County Recorder, County Surveyor and others in the Court House, Mary Jane was required to make numerous trips across the street.

In order to cross the street and do it without jaywalking Mary Jane had to walk to the Hopper and Myers Grocery Store and then turn left to use the crosswalk to the Court House Square. That took her to the corner with the drinking fountain. Often she'd pause for a cool drink of water.

Remember now, this is Bob Waddell's story.

"I wasn't always the nice quiet man of refinement people perceive me to be today. I used to wear a straw sailor's hat, white shoes, spats. Why, you might even say I looked like a bit of a dandy! Did you know I used to play the snare drums in the band with your Uncle John? And, my car was as fast and fancy as any around. It had an extremely loud horn that got me in trouble more than once.

"On the day I wanted to tell you about, Mary Jane had just leaned over the fountain to quench her thirst when I rounded the corner in my car. She had her hands on the bowl and her back to me.

"When I was about ten feet from her, I hit the horn button! Ted, you'll remember Mary Jane's size as large, like in L A R G E? In spite of that, when my horn blared out right behind her, she attempted to vault right over the fountain! She only made it half way!

"When I looked back to see what the effect of my loud horn blast had been, I instantly realized her predicament.

"I quickly pulled my car in beside the hitching rack--stopped-jumped out-and ran back to the fountain. With some sort of superhuman effort, I lifted Mary Jane off the drinking fountain.

"AND, did she thank me? No-o-o-o-o! Instead, she cussed me out good and then flounced off toward the Court House. Mad and wet!"

By that time, Bob was laughing so hard-remembering-his face was beet red and he was coughing.

"No more stories," he said. "My health can't take it, and besides, I have a lunch date with my favorite girl. My wife. Come see me again when we can talk longer."

I surely do treasure the couple of hours we spent together and I'm sorry I didn't go back to continue our conversation. I had a lot of questions that won't get answered, now. You see, he died just a few weeks later.

Did it again, didn't I? Got sidetracked.

It was early in the spring of 1932. Dad and I had been shearing sheep and on the way home he decided to stop at Fishers Cigar Store. Told me to wait in the car. We were parked right in front of the cigar store and in just a little while I could tell Dad had decided to stay for a while.

Nine year old boys don't like to sit quietly in a car by themselves. Don't now and never did. Never will.

There was some activity across the street next to the water fountain. Five or six boys were milling around laughing. I couldn't tell what they were doing and I decided to get out of the car and go see for myself. Not too much later I was wishing I hadn't been so curious. It was another time I had cause to remember Mama's saying, "Curiosity killed the cat."

"What are you boy's laughing at?" I asked in my friendliest tone of voice. They were all about my age, but I didn't know any of them.

"They're all laughing at the funny smell of my flower." The one boy said, with a very straight face. He didn't introduce himself, but I later found out his name was Eugene Marks. He wore glasses. I hadn't ever seen a boy who wore glasses. Matter of fact, Mary Lucille Seaney was the only girl I ever knew who wore glasses. I had always thought playing the piano had caused her to need them.

Anyway ...

Eugene said, "You want to smell my flower?"

A large daisy looking flower was protruding from the button hole of his shirt pocket. I thought it was pretty and I'd always liked the smell of flowers. So-I leaned over to smell his flower. That's when he squeezed the bulb and nearly drowned me! I'm serious! The water went, with some force, right up my nose! I choked, hacked, coughed and sneezed until I could get my breath again.

Then I did something very uncharacteristic of me. I grabbed the flower and gave it a big yank. The hose came loose from the rubber bulb in his pocket and I suddenly had the flower and about two feet of rubber hose in my hand.

I stood there, in front of him, and tore the hose into little pieces.

That's when he hit me in the nose. Boy, did that ever hurt! And bleed? For sure!

My first retaliatory swipe at Eugene knocked his glasses off. For a good half hour, we punched and wrestled each other until we were across the street and under the hitching racks alongside the bank building. That's where we did the most damage to each other. Those iron racks are very solid.

We'd attracted quite a crowd, including Sheriff John Luttman. His immediate assessment was that we weren't hurting each other. All that in spite of our torn clothes and bloody faces. So, he just watched with everybody else and cheered us on. There seldom was any excitement in LaGrange.

Dad finally got wind of what was going on and came out to put a stop to the fight. He had some very unkind things to say to Sheriff Luttman, but I think he was actually proud of me.

My first real fight! I think it was a draw. Eugene and I later became good friends and I don't think we ever fought again.

38

A Matter of Conscience

"An open foe may prove a curse
But a pretended friend is worse"
John Gay

No truer words were ever spoken!

I'd like to be able to say I've never had an open foe—or a pretended friend-but I can't. I've had both and I'd have to agree with John Gay, "A pretended friend is worse."

Lending money is one of the quickest ways to find out who your pretended friends are. I honestly believe in the sign I once saw which read, "Lending money makes enemies. Let's be friends." None the less, I've fallen for more than one sad story and, in the process, lost some friends. Well—actually—most everybody pays me back.

I hadn't intended to get started rambling about what happens when one lends money to his friends, so I won't. Instead, I want to talk to you about "conscience."

Everybody is born with a conscience. Whether or not we hone our conscience to a fine edge or let it become callused depends a good deal on our "fetchin' up." You know. What kind of conscience our parents had.

Often we hear the remark, "An apple doesn't fall far from the tree," or, "As the twig is bent, so grows the tree." Those are good rules of thumb but not necessarily true in every case. Sometimes, even the finest of parents will have one or more children who tend to resist their parents' best efforts to raise them as model citizens.

On the other hand, there are young ones who fortunately have the knack of selectively picking out, and following, only the best points of their parents. And grandparents can be role models, too.

Let me give you an example.

Price Jordan Jr. and I have been close business associates for nearly 15 years. Some while back a group of people made him a highly attractive offer to buy his business. The deal sounded fantastic! But-there was a catch. They wanted to continue using his name in the business.

After some soul searching—very little, in fact—Price refused their offer. Why? Because he was afraid they wouldn't treat his customers right and the integrity of his family name might become suspect. Price doesn't quote much scripture, but he believes strongly in what it says at Proverbs 22:1, "A name is to be chosen rather than abundant riches;" and at Ecclesiastes 7:1 where it says, "A name is better than good oil." I firmly believe that Price Jordan is the most honest used car dealer and garage owner that I've ever known. Bar none!

I don't know Price's dad but I know a couple of stories about his Granddad I'd like to tell.

Price's grandfather was a fairly influential man in the community back before many roads were paved and only a few were black topped.

I'm talking about Fort Bend County, Texas, now.

Came a time when the County Commissioners had to decide which of two roads were to be black topped. To determine the automobile usage of these two roads, they had put those rubber hoses across the roads to count the cars that went by. Here came the neighbors to "influential" grandpa. "We want our road surfaced! We're tired of the dust from this shell road. Help us! You have influence with the County Commissioners!

Not wanting to let them down and wanting the better road himself, grandpa took his car and, after dark and virtually all traffic had stopped moving, he drove to the spot where the counter was located. Then, for a half hour, he drove over the counter. And, drove over the counter. Forward and backward. He kept it up for a half hour.

Then he drove the short distance to home and bed.

And, was he able to sleep? NO! Instead, he tossed and turned until 2:30 in the morning when he got up, put on his clothes, and drove the 14 miles to the traffic counter on the other road. There, with his finely honed conscience in control, he drove back and forth across this counter for a half hour.

Then, he drove 14 miles home to bed where he slept soundly with a clear conscience.

Price told me he was tremendously influenced by something else his grandpa did.

"Grandpa was considered to be reasonably affluent. In other words, he was fairly well off financially. He could have, had he wanted, bought a new car every year. But, he didn't really drive all that many miles and it seemed a real waste of money. So, for years, when his car's speedometer showed 24,000 miles, he made plans to get rid of it and buy a new car.

"'By the time I get the car ready to sell, it'll have close to 25,000 miles on it and that's far enough to have driven once around the world. Time to get rid of it.' That was my grandpa.

"Before he set it out front with a 'For Sale' sign on it, he'd have all the dents repaired, paint chips painted and the car washed until it looked like new. He'd have it greased, oil and all filters and belts changed, and then he'd put on a new set of good tires. Last thing was a tune up.

"'I never want anybody to say I sold them a car that wasn't in good condition.'

"Ted, that's always been my philosophy, too. I never want a used car to leave our lot that isn't in as good condition as we can make it." And, I believe it. For him, it's a matter of conscience.

Of course-it reminds me of something that happened during the Great Depression.

Dad didn't have any skills except farming and we'd already lost the farm.

Most of the time, he tried hard to find work even if it was only for one day at a time. Or, even a few hours. He sheared sheep in the spring. Anything, to make a dollar or even less.

Then came the time he was offered $2.00 for just a few hours work and he refused. It was a matter of conscience.

Dad was in Fishers Cigar Store, just loafing and talking with old friends, when Sheriff John Luttman came in. "I'm looking for some able bodied men to help me set John Smith's furniture and belongings out along the road in front of his house. I'll pay each man $2.00. Who wants to work?"

"What happened, Sheriff? Why are you moving John out?"

"He can't pay his taxes and the state's foreclosing."

In those days two dollars was a lot of money but, in unison, they all said, "Throw him off his farm yourself, John. We're not going to kick a friend while he's down!"

It was a matter of conscience.

39

Grandmother's Chair

My mother was an inveterate story teller and, once she heard one she liked, she seldom forgot it. People enjoyed telling her stories because she was a good listener. By that, I mean she laughed heartily at a good story. For a fact, it's more fun to tell a story to someone who laughs easily.

Mother read to us, too. That fact caused my sister Edie to send me the following note:

"Wish I could say I wrote this—but I found it somewhere—thought you'd like it."

You might have tangible wealth untold,
Caskets of jewels and coffers of gold,
But richer than I you can never be,
'Cause I had a mother who read to me.

How true that is. I'm convinced that children who are read to when they are very young, or even before they are born, wind up being excellent readers themselves. At least, the chances are better.

Good readers normally have a better than average command of "The King's English." Studies have shown that worldwide, the most successful people are those who have the ability to speak fluent and correct English.

Back in the 20's and 30's, before television and even before virtually everybody had a radio, story telling was a way of life. It was an art cultivated by many. Now, to find a good story teller is a rarity.

My mother had a whole string of "story" songs she used to sing. My sister Mary sent me this old English ditty. It was one of

Mom's favorites. I don't remember what tune she sang it to, but here it is:

Grandmother's Chair

1st verse
My grandmother she, at the age of 83
One day in May was taken ill and died.
And after she was dead the will of course was read
By the lawyer as we all sat by his side.
To my brother it was found she had left 100 pounds.
And the same to my sister I declare.
But when it came to me the lawyer said, I see
She has left you her old arm chair.

Chorus
How they tittered, how they chaffed
How my brother and my sister laughed
When they heard the lawyer declare
Granny only left to you her old arm chair.

2nd verse
Well, I didn't think it fair but I said I didn't care
And in the eve I took the chair away
While my sister at me laughed
And my brother at me chaffed.
And they said, it will come in handy, John.
When you settle down in life some day,
With some girl to be your wife
You'll find it rather handy, I declare
On a cold and stormy night when the fire is burning bright
You can then sit in your old arm chair!

Chorus

3rd verse
What my brother said was true for in a year or two
Strange to say I settled down in married life.
I first the girl did court and then the ring I bought.

Then I took her to the Church to be my wife.
The old girl and me were as happy as could be
And strange to say I never cared to roam,
but each night I stayed at home
And was seated in my old arm chair.

Chorus

4th verse
Well, one night the chair fell down
And when I picked it up I found
The seat had fallen out upon the floor
And there to my surprise I saw before my eyes
A lot of notes, 10, 000 pounds or more!
When my brother heard of this the fellow I confess
Near went wild with rage and tore at his hair.
But I only laughed at him and I said unto him,
Don't you wish you had the old arm chair?

Chorus
How they tittered, how they chaffed
How my brother and my sister laughed
When they heard the lawyer declare
Granny only left to you her old arm chair.

And that was it.

Mom had a variety of readings and recitations she'd give at the slightest sign of an invitation.

I'd like to share a couple of her short stories, or jokes. She probably read them in an old magazine or, at least, somebody told them to her and she was repeating.

"Did you hear the one about the lady who married four times? She first married a millionaire, then an actor, then a preacher, and lastly, an undertaker.

"One for the money, two for the show, three to make ready, and four to go."

If you think that's bad, read on.

"Paw," said the farmer's boy, I want to go to college and study to be a Doctor. I think I'll study obstetrics."

"Like as not you'll be wastin' your time, son," replied the father. "Soon as you learn about that 'obstetrics,' somebody'll come along with a cure."

That was my Mama. She had a delightful sense of humor.

40

Carl Dintaman, Son of George

My brother, Lloyd, had a host of friends and I'm finding that they never tire of talking about him. If you'd compare his friends to an ocean, his enemies wouldn't fill a milk bucket. I'm going to excerpt a letter from Carl Dintaman, one of Lloyd's life long friends. He told me many things about himself, in this letter, of which I was unaware. It pleased me for him to say that he approved of the story I had written about his father, George Dintaman.

"I especially liked the paragraph where you said, 'George Dintaman was a subscriber to the theory that success is a journey, not a destination.' You said, too, that he had indoctrinated me with the same philosophy. It has, indeed, been a journey for me and my family.

"In 1939, my wife Salena and I took over the operation of Dad's farm. I'm talking about the old Slack homestead. At that time, Mother and Dad moved across the road to the old Joseph Merrifield farm. You've mentioned George Grantham and his wife, Barbara. He was the minister at the Bethel Church.

"They moved out of the parsonage in the spring of 1931 and onto the Merrifield's farm. He preached and farmed and helped other farmers -threshing, etc. My folks moved onto that farm when the Granthams left.

"After Salina and I were married it seemed like only a few years until we had six little helpers. They were our children, Phillip, Phyllis, Carol, Carl Jr., Stephen, and Pamela. They certainly did their share in making our farming journey a success. The 'success' included adding a considerable number of acres to the original farm.

"Ted, in going back 60 years, when you, Lloyd, and myself were boys on Bethel-Saylor road, it doesn't look the same. The

Dintaman name is still on the mail box, but not so names like Chrystler, Hart, Olmstead, Eaton, Latta, Parsons, Lynch, Springer, McCally, McKibben, Bogue, Merrifield, Walters, Bear, Dunithan—now take a breath—Giggy, Krugh, Bradley, Gottschalk, Slack, Burgi, Woodworth, etc.

"I believe the Bethel Church held it's last service in 1949, although the building is still there. The last funerals I remember attending there were Emmet Krugh, Toby Chrystler and Mrs. Otis Hart.

"This area of Bethel Church and Saylor School has completely changed. Virtually all the old, narrow, gravel roads you write about are gone. Replaced, in most cases, by reasonably wide blacktop roads.

"The old, wooden, white, Saylor School house is gone, but there are three Amish schools within a mile of our place. One is located one mile west, another is one mile east, and another one mile south. I have many Amish neighbors and friends. I feel at home with my Amish neighbors and they seem to accept me, too.

"I'm not young any more and some day the Old Isaac Slack Homestead will be for sale. None of our sons or daughters chose to follow farming as an occupation. For that reason, approximately 18 years ago, we sold most of our land and farming equipment. We kept only the Old Slack Farm 80 acres where we live.

"The past 52 years, farming has been a journey—no question about it. Shortly after my wife and I took up the farming operation from my Dad, Rufus Yoder and Mel Weber encouraged us to raise popcorn. Compared to other crops, popcorn was a good price, but the ears were so small it seemed like it took forever to get a wagonload.

"I decided there had to be an easier way to harvest popcorn than to husk it by hand. Why not use a corn picker? I had an almost new New Idea Corn Picker and suggested to Rufus that we try it on popcorn. His answer was, 'It won't work! You can try it if you like but it won't work.' Dad's comment was, 'You'll never know if you don't try.' We tried it. It worked! By some careful adjustment of the picking apparatus, it worked and worked well.

"I delivered Rufus his first popcorn picked with a corn picker. The fact of the matter is, we not only harvested our own popcorn but, for several years, we harvested the popcorn raised on the farms of both Rufus Yoder and Mel Weber.

"Yoder's popcorn is now famous throughout the country. Rufus' son, Larry, is still operating the plant over 50 years later.

"After the children left the farm I decided to slow down. I couldn't imagine retiring, at least not completely, so we put most of our land to grass and just fed cattle on these farms.

"Most of our cattle were bought and sold through the Shipshewana Auction ever since I can remember. I'd like to pay tribute to some of the men who have given me, as well as the whole community, a good market for livestock.

"They would include George Curtis, Fred Lambright, Walter Shrock, and Lambright and Sons.

"I owe a great debt of gratitude, as well, to my parents and my children. And, my wives. I've been doubly blessed in having two wonderful helpmates.

Salina, the mother of our children, died. I missed her very much but the single life was not for me, so I remarried. Now, when tourists stop to take pictures of Rosalie and the flowers in our front yard, I know they really want a picture of her.

"In addition to the flowers, when you go by our farm home, you'll probably see cattle in the fields. I still feed some cattle. There's not much profit because, although I raise hay for them, I buy the rest of their feed. But, it gives me something to keep me busy. I still try to do a good job of maintaining the buildings, fences, and the yard.

"Yes, Ted, I am still living in the Old Isaac Slack Homestead. Recently, I was walking through the cemetery across the road from Bethel Church. There I found the headstone marking the grave of Isaac Slack. It indicated that he died in 1889. Buried beside him is Anna, his wife. Close by are Carter, Ella, Mary, and Orlando Slack.

"Buried beside the Slacks are William and Barbara Saylor. This is the couple who donated the land for the cemetery and after whom the Saylor School is named.

"Yes, Ted, I miss your brother. Lloyd and I were always very close. When he stayed with you and Cecil at the parsonage he'd often come down and help me with chores, etc. My mother always insisted he stay for a meal. He gladly accepted. Times were hard for the family when you lived at the Bethel Parsonage.

"Lloyd and I rode horses and mules together. Lloyd helped me break a Bronco Western Horse. That horse could really buck, but Lloyd kept at it until the bronco was finally rideable. I'd hate to have to guess how many times he 'bit the dust' before the horse gave in to him. Lloyd was a determined one.

"Lloyd and I double dated together. Sometimes, after the date, I'd take him to your Uncle Bela's house over on North Twin Lake.

"I remember some of Lloyd's songs. When riding in my pickup or car at times I sing them—I did just the other day.

"A couple of years ago my wife, Rosalie, had Lloyd's and Maurice Davis's here for dinner. Lloyd and Maurice and I spent the afternoon talking about the good times we had together when we were boys and in our early 20's."

Yes, Carl, I miss Lloyd, too.

41

How to Show Love to Your Children

Have you ever watched a child spend time playing with an empty box that had contained some household appliance? The empty box didn't cost anything but a child, with an active imagination, can convert it to an airplane, a secret club house, a fort, or even a cave. Imagination, that's all it takes. And, I'm speaking about during times of plenty when most children have an abundance of toys to play with.

During the depression days, toys were few and far between. Store bought toys, that is. We didn't have many toys of the store bought or homemade variety. At our house I remember having the short and the long sticks needed to play the game of zippy. Pieces of a broom handle is what they were. And, Dad had a horse shoe pit with the stakes and the shoes needed to play. Neither game is much fun when you're by yourself. That's a good part of the reason why I spent so many hours with the Ed Shrock family. There I had playmates.

At the time, I thought the year we spent living at the parsonage, and my going to Saylor School, was the loneliest time of my life. It might have been but, looking back at it now, I did have a few friends and that helped. Ed and Fannie Shrock spent a considerable amount of quality time with their children. I'm convinced that their spending so much time together made them love each other more. And, it didn't really matter if they were working together or playing together.

During the winter there was school during the day but milking and other chores to be done in the barn in the evening. Spring and summer meant no school but plenty of work, all day long, in the fields, together. Theirs was not an all work and no play existence. Far from it. But, there were no store bought toys or games. Ed was almost ingenious in his ability to produce homemade entertainment. And, he enjoyed playing games with the children. This was "togetherness" in its best form. Let me tell you about some of the games and toys he made.

Mr. Shrock built a miniature croquet set. Everything had to be placed on the dining room table. This meant the wire arches couldn't be driven into anything. They had to be free standing. This just meant using longer pieces of wire and more bending. But, he did it. He made the little croquet mallets and marbles were used for balls. It was very intricate and took a long time to make. It provided many enjoyable hours of entertainment.

Gears from an old clock made excellent tops. By holding the shaft between your thumb and index finger, and making sort of a snapping motion, the wheel would spin like a top. Mr. Shrock would keep time with the second hand on his big gold pocket watch in order to determine the winner of the longest spin.

And then there were spools. Back in those days women had a regular day for patching, mending, and darning.

Dresses and such were often homemade and so there was a considerable amount of sewing. For those reasons, empty thread spools were in ample supply for young ones to use for making toys. Girls made dolls with them and boys made cars with all they could get hold of.

Mr. Shrock showed us how to make an automatic automobile using rubber bands, soap, and a couple of sticks.

My memory says the whole thing was simply a match stick through a rubber band, then the rubber band through the spool. Next a piece of wafer thin soap cut like a washer with a hole in the middle. The rubber band extends on through the soap. A longer stick is then pushed through and used to wind-up the rubber band until it's tight. Just put it on a flat surface and it'll slowly move as the rubber band unwinds.

Checkers! They played checkers! That's not at all unusual but this game was. Mr. Shrock painted the checker board design on a square piece of lumber. Wait'll I tell you how he made the checkers! He sawed 24 quarter inch thick pieces from an old broom stick using a hand saw. Half of them he painted red and the other half he painted black. And there you have it-a home made checker board and checkers.

Another "educational" game he made was nothing more than a big board in which he had driven long nails at irregular intervals. It might have been an old door, I don't remember. Below each nail was written a number. Using ten rubber fruit rings, the object was to ring as many of the nails as possible. We always tried to ring the biggest numbers because the winner was the one with the highest total score.

What we children didn't think of, at the time, was that Ed and Fannie were helping us learn to add. I, for one, needed all the help I could get and now I appreciate their assistance.

Ed Shrock believed there was evil in the face cards of a regulation deck of playing cards. I'm not at all sure he wasn't right. So, here's what they did:

Although it was a bit of a luxury, Fannie would buy an occasional box of Post Toasties. My memory says the corn flakes came in only one size-HUGE! When the box was emptied it was not discarded. Rather, it was cut into playing card size and shape pieces. Then, when enough boxes had been saved to make 52 cards, names were put on the blank side of these pieces of cardboard. Bible names. The Shrocks wanted their children to know the Bible and the names of the various people mentioned. What better way than to play cards with Bible names rather than numbers or Jacks, Queens, Kings, or Aces on them?

So the game of Books could be played, a name such as Abraham would be written on four of the cards. On four more, the name Joseph might have been used. And so on, until 13 sets were made up. The game was fun, interesting and educational.

Ed and Fannie Shrock knew how to show love to their children and I'm glad they were my friends and neighbors.

42

Fried Chicken With All the Trimmings
At the Merrill Eaton Farm
Oh! How I Loved It!

Vera and Merrill Eaton were well known for their hospitality. Their active participation in the activities of the Bethel Church was one of the cords that held the congregation together. They considered it their Christian duty to give a helping hand to "widows and orphans," and a whole passel of others who were neither.

It was on land owned by Josiah Eaton that the Saylor School was built. Josiah owned approximately 200 acres of land on the south side of the road, where Saylor School was located, and 80 acres on the north side. The east fork of Buck Creek ran through those acres as did the Old Valley Line Railroad.

Early history of Clay Township shows that my Great-Great-Great-Grandfather, Eppah Robbins, built the first blacksmith shop in the area on the banks of Buck Creek, close to what was later known as Fleck's Mill Pond.

The dam, built on the north end of the pond, served a dual purpose. It furnished water power for the old saw mill, built in 1837, and the new combination saw and grist mill, built in 1867 by Emanuel Fleck. That's where the name, Fleck's Mill Pond, came from. In addition, the dam served as a bridge in order for the Old Valley Line Railroad to cross Buck Creek. Oh, yes! The dam also helped make a very nice swimming hole for the Eaton kids and earlier ones.

There's a considerable amount of interesting history associated with this corner of Clay Township. For instance, the Old Valley Line Railroad seems to have cut between the Saylor Cemetery and the Bethel Church, thence across the front of Isaac Slack's and Samuel Crowl's farms. Then it moved on past the rear of Everett School heading west.

The great Massachusetts lawyer-statesman, The Honorable Daniel Webster, bought the 80 acres of land a half mile directly north of the Bethel Church on July 20, 1836. He later sold it to Senator James A. Bayard. Now I ask you, isn't that interesting?

How about this? A mile directly east of the parcel of land formerly owned by Daniel Webster was a section or more of marsh land owned by Joshua T. Hobbs and known as Hobbs Marsh. In the early times, bog iron ore, or limonite, was obtained from Hobb's Marsh. This iron was utilized by works built especially for that purpose near Lima, now known as Howe. This business soon proved unprofitable and closed down.

Back to Fleck's Mill for a second. I'd nearly forgotten, but I once had a school mate named Floyd Fleck. I wonder if his great-grandfather might not have been "Emanuel Fleck." H-m-m-m. You suppose? For that matter, I wonder what ever happened to my friend, Floyd Fleck.

Back to my original subject, "Fried chicken, etc."

Charles came up to me as school was letting out and said, "Vera told me I could invite you to stop for supper. Do you want to?" Charles lived with the Eatons.

"Do I want to? Does a cat have claws? Of course I want to!" I couldn't contain my exuberance!

"Take it easy, Ted! And, try to act like you had good sense, tonight. Also, watch your manners at the supper table." Charles was afraid I was going to embarrass him. I knew that if I did it wouldn't be the first time and probably not the last. Charles tended to be quiet and reserved, especially around older folks. I wasn't what you'd call brash but I sure wasn't quiet or reserved.

I tried to hurry Charles and Robert on the way to Robert's house. It didn't do me any good because as usual, on the farm, chores had to be done first. Neither of them were in any big hurry to get home and start working. Admittedly, I kind of enjoyed helping with chores. I'd always liked animals and feeding calves that had been taken away from their mothers was one of my favorites. Another was, for some unknown reason, I got a big kick out of slopping hogs and watching them eat until they had their fill. Maybe I got some sort of satisfaction in watching somebody, or something, get plenty to eat.

I didn't like to milk cows. Couldn't seem to successfully get the hang of it. But, I thought turning the crank on the cream separator was real fun and entertaining. I liked the almost musical sound of the mechanism itself. And, to watch the milk coming out one pipe and the cream out of another was purely magical.

After all the farm animals were fed, the milking done, and the cream separated, it was time to wash up for supper. That's what I had really been looking forward to. Supper!

Vera had invited me to supper so she obviously knew I would be there, but I couldn't believe my eyes when I saw the table. It was set for Sunday dinner! My mouth hung open and I'm just sure I drooled while I inhaled the tantalizing odors. My eyes nearly popped out of their sockets as I gazed with hungry anticipation on a table full of food including a huge platter of steaming, fried chicken, and all the trimmings.

It was as though I was floating along in a dream when Charles brought me down to earth with, "Ted! Sit down! Everybody's waiting for you!" Only then did I realize I was standing there just staring at the delicious looking food.

We all sat quietly as Merrill asked the blessing. The boys, Robert, Glendon, and little Daryle, all bowed their heads.

The first thing passed, after the Amen, was the chicken. When Charles, who was sitting on my right, handed me the platter, my first inclination was to look for the neck. But, I didn't because there was plenty for everybody to even have seconds. I took a drumstick. Right away, Charles passed me the mashed potatoes. I helped myself and passed them on. Immediately, I took a bite of the fried chicken. M-m-m-m, it was good. Then Charles tried to pass me the chicken gravy. I quickly took another bite of my drumstick before I accepted the gravy boat.

"There's plenty for everybody, Ted! You don't have to eat like a pig." I'd embarrassed Charles again. This would probably be the last time I'd be invited for supper.

"Now, Charles. You let the boy alone. He's just hungry." Vera was coming to my defense and I did get invited again.

Really, the meal was outstanding, or, at least I thought so. English peas, beets, Swiss chard, baking powder biscuits right after the mashed potatoes. Following Merrill's lead, I broke the hot biscuit in two next to the potatoes, then poured the gravy over both the potatoes and the biscuits. Something else. There was fresh churned butter and strawberry jam for the biscuits, too. Of course, a big glass of milk.

Then, guess what? She had baked huckleberry pie for dessert. I had eaten so much I was literally stuffed, but every boy's stomach always has room for a piece of pie.

I really loved Vera and Merrill Eaton.

43

A Dinner You'll Never Forget

Even though it meant I had to turn the crank of the shearing machine all day long, I looked forward to the times Dad had a job shearing some farmers sheep. The farmers wife had to furnish our dinner. That was part of the deal. Ten cents a head and our dinner. If I live to be a hundred, and I intend to, I'll never forget the time when we sheared the sheep of a farmer named Marvin Snow.

Marvin Snow's farm did not have the appearance of being one of the more successful farming operations. On the contrary, the house and all of the other buildings needed a coat or two of paint. Some of the smaller out buildings looked in danger of collapse. Pieces of old dilapidated farm machinery, with tall dead weeds grown up through them, stood in a small grove of ragged trees. To put it mildly, it did not conjure up a look of success.

The whole picture was as a centennial farm whose buildings had not felt the stroke of a paint brush since the day they had been built a hundred years before.

Mr. Snow came out the back door of the house to greet us as we drove the old Model T into the yard. Dad knew him so they shook hands as soon as Dad got out of the car. To me, Mr. Snow looked old and tired. He seemed to brighten up some as he and Dad stood for a while and talked. Dad's smile was infectious. Maybe it was at least partly because of his gold-filled front tooth. It gave him a really bright smile.

"We've been expecting you," Mr. Snow said, talking to us both. "My wife has planned a dinner you'll never forget."

"That's sounds good to me." I said. Dad thought so, too, and said as much with another big smile. He liked almost any kind of food and drink. Mom said he had a cast-iron stomach.

Mr. Snow had the ewes and one really big buck sheep penned in the part of the barn that had the horse stalls. In two of the stalls he had penned in 25 or 30 lambs. He didn't have that many ewes which meant there had to be several sets of twins. Multiple births are not that unusual from Shropshire ewes, especially with a big healthy buck sheep being the sire.

The lambs were really crowded together in the two stalls. Then, at almost the same time, Dad and I noticed something unusual. The lambs still had their tails!

"Well, I'll declare, Marvin! These lambs still have their tails!" Dad was talking. Normally, the tails would have been cut off a month before. These lambs were pretty good-sized already. "And, why do you have them penned up in here? You want us to shear 'em?" Dad laughed nervously at his own joke. You don't shear lambs.

Mr. Snow laughed, too. "No. I don't want you to shear them." He was much more serious now. "I would appreciate it if you and Ted would cut their tails off. I couldn't do it by myself and I didn't want to ask my daughter to help me."

"Well, all right, Marvin. We'll take care of it." Dad wasn't too happy about it.

"There is one other thing, Cecil. The male lambs haven't been castrated. I'd like you and Ted to do that, too." Mr. Snow seemed embarrassed to ask.

"Now, wait a minute! That'll take some time. We'll be hard-pressed just to shear all these sheep today. I don't want to have to come back tomorrow." Dad was clearly upset.

"I'll pay you extra to do it." Mr. Snow was pleading by now.

"Pay!" The magic word. He had Dad's undivided attention.

"It'll cost you five cents a head!" That was half as much as we got for shearing each one of the sheep. I'm sure Dad didn't expect Mr. Snow to agree, but he did.

"You've made a bargain! One other thing, though. You can just toss the tails into the straw, but I want you to put the testicles in a container that I'll bring for you."

"That's fine with me." They would have been a mess thrown into the straw around where we were going to work. Dad assumed he was going to feed them to the hogs, a common practice.

And, that's the way it was done. Dad figured it was a good deal because we could do two lambs a lot more quickly than we could shear one sheep. Mr. Snow helped, too. He lifted each one of the lambs out of their pen and handed them to me. I held them while Dad performed his "veterinary" work. When we finished, Mr. Snow carried the container out with him, the one with the testicles, that is.

It was after 1:00 before Mr. Snow came to tell us dinner was ready. We both were famished. Dad said, "I could eat a horse."

After we had washed up, we sat down at the table. Only three places had been set. The mother and daughter just waited on the three of us.

"What an unusual assortment of food," I thought. Everything was white, or nearly so. No green. There were mashed potatoes, white gravy, cauliflower, and white sweet corn. Almost spooky! And then, there was this platter of fried meat. It looked like rather small pieces of round steak. Dad and I thought it looked scrumptious. Steak and potatoes! We dug right in.

After every dish had been passed around and we had helped ourselves, we ate in silence until Dad spoke up.

"What kind of meat is this, Marvin? It's delicious." Dad had a very pleased look on his face.

Mr. Snow answered, "It's called 'mountain oysters'. I'm glad you like them."

"Is that so? Well, I declare! This is some of the best meat I've ever eaten." I thought so, too.

For dessert we had custard pie. Their cooking sure leaned toward light colored foods but it was good.

After dinner, Dad and I headed back for the barn. We still had a substantial amount of work to do. Just as Dad was about to catch the first ewe, so we could get started shearing, he stopped and said to me, "I hated to expose my ignorance, but I still don't know what that meat was. I don't suppose you know what 'mountain oysters' are?"

"Sure, Dad. They're what you pulled out of those male lambs."

Almost instantly, Dad turned white as a sheet. He opened his mouth and the most horrified look of shock came over his face. He grabbed his throat with both hands and made a retching sound. Then he suddenly leaned over forward and started to vomit. He lost it all.

So much for Dad's "cast iron" stomach.

44

Raising a Garden at the Parsonage

Back in the 1930's, the one-room, one-teacher country schools let out for summer vacation on May first, come rain or come shine. "Four months of carefree fun and games for the kids," you say?

"No! four months of helping Dad on the farm" was the lot of most farm children. May through August were the plowing, planting, cultivating, and harvesting months on the farm. Cash crop time.

Dad never did any farming after the bank foreclosed on the farm where I was born. Well, that is, no farming except for keeping a big garden and he did that almost all the rest of his life, even at the Parsonage. Although I worked some in the garden I didn't have to work all summer on the farm until the second year after we moved from the parsonage.

It seemed like Dad was on the prowl every day for whatever kind of work he could get. The only reasonably steady jobs he had were shearing sheep in the early spring and working at Robbin's Creamery during the summer months. Uncle John and Aunt Eleanor Robbins owned the creamery. You know something?

I can't remember if they made butter from the cream they bought or if they sold it to one of the big butter companies. What I do remember is that the place always smelled of sour cream. The floors throughout the building were concrete. Aunt Ellen was forever mopping the floor, so it was always wet.

There was another odor that wasn't easy to forget. They bought and dressed a lot of chickens. Freshly butchered chickens have an aroma all their own. I think maybe the smell of wet chicken feathers came through over all the other odors.

I remember they sold ice cream, too. Aunt Ellen regularly gave me ice cream cones.

Ellen wasn't really my Aunt. John Robbins was my father's cousin, a couple of times removed. No matter. They seemed like Aunt Ellen and Uncle John to me. Their daughters, Willowdeane and Violet, were like older cousins and I guess that's what they were. Several times removed. I sure liked them a lot. They used to give me a free ice cream cone from time to time, too.

That's the only way I'd have gotten one.

And ice! They sold ice and used a lot of it in their creamery. They didn't make ice, but bought it from an ice plant in Sturgis. Dad and Hansel Wallace used to haul ice for them and then they'd both work in the creamery. I rode with them to Sturgis with some regularity in the summer. It seemed like an awfully long trip. It was twelve miles.

In the recesses of my memory I can see Dad and Hansel Wallace erecting a sign alongside the road between LaGrange and Howe. It must have been an extra job that Hansel picked up. I can't remember too much about it except that they put the posts into two already existing holes in the ground. Actually, the holes weren't already there. The remains of an old sign was there. Two broken legs of an old sign would be more like it. The old sign was lying in the tall grass and weeds. Dad and Hansel pushed the legs, or posts, back and forth until they were loose enough so they could pull them out of the ground. It wasn't too hard to do because the sign was located in kind of a low spot just inside the fence. Farmers didn't like to let anybody put signs up in an area that could be plowed easily.

And, the sign they put up advertised Carl Rehm's Clothing Store. At the time, Carl Rehm's was the finest men's clothing store in Sturgis and may very well still be.

The sign was at least eight feet wide and four feet high. The bottom of the sign was probably six feet from the ground. I thought it was truly magnificent and I was proud of my Dad and Hansel.

In later much more prosperous years I became acquainted with Carl Rehm and bought a considerable amount of my clothes from his store. Somehow, I felt a kinship to him. Like, maybe, my Dad had helped contribute to his success in business. Likely Dad never met Carl Rehm.

Another memory just popped into my mind and I'll tell you about it:

It may have happened only two or three times but I remember the first time Hansel deviated from the direct route to the Ice Plant. He pulled the truck up into the driveway of a house I'd never seen before.

"I've got some business I want to transact with the man who lives here. Cecil, you come in with me. Ted, you stay in the truck." With that, they both walked up onto the porch of the house. A man opened the door and they both walked on inside. I waited.

Although it may have been 15 or 20 minutes, it seemed like at least an hour before they emerged. They were talking and laughing and their faces were flushed. They smelled funny, too. Eventually, I was to discover what "home-brew" smelled like and how it can make a change in one's personality.

But, let's get back to gardening!

There's an old saying that "You can take the boy off the farm, but you can't take the farm out of the boy." Although Dad lost the farm, he kept a big garden wherever he lived. He did that until he was at least 90 years old. It helped keep him alive. It benefited him physically, financially, and mentally. It acted as a form of therapy. I know it works. I keep a big garden every summer.

Dad was convinced he'd surely die if he didn't eat potatoes at least twice a day. He favored three times a day. For that reason, the big garden plot out behind was an attraction when we rented the parsonage for $3.00 per month.

Early in the spring, Dad asked Ed Shrock to plow up this approximately half an acre patch. Ed did a good job of it. After he finished dragging, the field was ready to plant. Dad planted early potatoes first, of course. Red ones. Dad liked early red potatoes and English peas, so he planted peas at the same time. Tomato seeds were put into the ground early, too.

Later, Dad planted Swiss chard, green beans, beets, carrots, sweet corn, and late potatoes. And, of course, he set out the tomato plants. Mom had plenty of canning to do on the weekends she came home from work at the County Infirmary. Dad and I had

164

plenty of vegetables for use all summer. Most importantly, we had an ample supply of potatoes to last all summer and winter.

We wouldn't have wanted Dad to die for lack of potatoes. Now, would we?

45

The Robbins Family Reunion—1932

"Mama! Why do we always go to the Robbins family reunion? We're Woodworth's!"

Now mind you, I wasn't complaining about going someplace where there would be lots of good food and I'd get to see my cousin, June. No! It was just that nobody had ever bothered to explain it to me.

"Some of your Dad's relatives were named Robbins. You know John and Ellen Robbins. They own the creamery and ice house. Your Pa works for them, sometimes, delivering ice with Hansel Wallace. And, you know their daughters, Willowdeane and Violet."

"Sure I know them and they always come, but I don't know how we're related.'"

"They're your cousins! Now, hurry up and get ready."

Mama had fixed her special dish, baked dried corn. You'd have to taste it in order to appreciate it.

Navy beans had soaked all night long so she was able to fix a big dish of baked beans. To keep them from being dry, she used a lot of black strap sorghum molasses and brown sugar. Ummmm!

We had enough dried navy beans, up in the attic, to last our whole family the rest of our lives. Or so it seemed. Actually, they only lasted another ten or twelve years.

But that's another story.

I'm in favor of reunions. Often as not it's the only time you get to see some of your relatives. Most assuredly, I think one should get to know all their relatives. And then again, young folks don't always ask questions and so chances are they never find out how some of the reunion attendees are related to them.

For instance, I never knew how William and Emma Walterspaugh were related to us. Some others were Nelson Milliman, Jesse Healy, Bert Winans, Maurice Hecht and Dr. and Mrs. W. 0. Hildebrand. I should have asked but I didn't. And how about M.F. and Sarah Crandell, Sears Price, Lester Fair and Joseph Prough? A few more I couldn't reconcile to the family tree were Ashley and Nora Ritter, Mary Jane Somborger, Mr. and Mrs. Ora Bingham and Dexter Bingham. Fred, Claude, and Francis Auten were just part of the Auten family that attended. Francis Auten played the guitar and the mouth harp. There were Nedra and Penny Nichols. I didn't know how we were related but I liked their names.

There was an Armstrong family, too. I liked for them to come because they had two boys about my age. Harry was almost exactly my age and Robert was younger. There was an older boy and a daughter named Elmira. She had a shock of flaming red hair. I think the boys did too, except Robert. His hair was black. Mrs. Armstrong's name was Alice and she gave great recitations that everyone looked forward to.

It was always a special treat when the Binghams brought their portable organ and their mandolin.

There was no shortage of talent in the family. Most of the children were good singers and then we had those who played the guitar, violin, mouth harp, Jews harp, and accordion. Audra Woodworth played the "squeeze box," and very well indeed. Her name is now Czajkowski.

Uncle James Woodworth was an auctioneer and he often entertained us by singing, whistling, saying tongue twisters or actually auctioning something to the highest bidder.

One of the several reasons we preferred having the reunion at the James Woodworth cottages was the proximity of Pigeon River. Uncle James had row boats for the renters and we rowed them up and down the river weaving in and out of any tree branches that extended down to the water. We pretended all kinds of adventures that ranged from hiding from Indians in our canoes to being aboard a pirate ship.

There were lots of shells in the shallow water, especially clam shells. Most everybody would tote away a basket clear full of shells and pretty rocks.

Picnic tables in the shade of huge maple trees seemed always to be blessed with cool breezes that appeared to follow along the river. It was a balmy place to spend an afternoon of reminiscing and getting reacquainted.

Here is the secretary's report for the reunion of 1932: "The tenth annual reunion of the Robbins family was held at the James Woodworth cottage on Pigeon River Sunday, August 28, 1932.

"The rain in the forenoon threatened to spoil the day, but regardless of the weather, 42 relatives gathered from far and near to enjoy the day together.

"Mr. & Mrs. Herman Lampman and son, from Huntington, Indiana, coming the greatest distance. This being the first reunion they had attended, their presence was greatly appreciated.

"At noon, all enjoyed the pot luck dinner served cafeteria-style.

"In the afternoon the men played horse shoes, the young folks went boat riding and the rest visited.

"Later, the president, Claude Auten, called the company together for the business meeting. The minutes of the previous reunion were read. It was moved and seconded that the old officers be retained. It was decided to have the next reunion at the same place the last Sunday in August. A collection of $1.26 was taken. $0.25 was paid for cards and the balance given to James Woodworth for coffee and lemons.

"We were then favored with several selections on the guitar and mouth harp by Francis Auten. Mrs. Alice Armstrong gave a reading and Mrs. Lampman a recitation. Ted Woodworth sang and Sylvia Woodworth gave a reading.

"After good-byes were said, each family departed feeling that they had spent a most pleasant time together."

Cleon Robbins, Secretary.

Let me tell you what I finally discovered my relationship to be with the Robbins family:

In the early 1800's, the Eppah Robbins family came from Pennsylvania and settled on the northwest corner of Pretty Prairie. They were among the first settlers. In 1836, they built the first blacksmith shop on the banks of Buck Creek, close to Fleck's Mill Pond, west and south of Howe, Indiana. The Eppah Robbins had six children, one of which was a son named John. This John Robbins married Sarah Davenport. They had eight children including a daughter named Melissa.

Melissa married Ira M. Woodworth. They had four children, Sarah (Crandell), Fayette R., Mary (Lampman) and Bela.

I can take it from there.

Fayette married Icey V. Green. Their seven children were Cecil, James, Beulah, Mary, McKinly, John and Bela.

Cecil married Sylvia Todd. Their six children were Edythe, Mary, Lloyd, Charles, Wayne and Ted.

Ted married Zena Schoen from Kansas. We are parents to Rebecka (Morse), Edythe (Hewgley) and Terry.

And now hear this! Those two girls have six children between them. Three of those six have seven children, total. Simply, Zena and I have three children, six grand-children and seven great-grand-children.

Where have all the years gone?

Ford V-8, Model 40, Victoria, Tudor Sedan

46

The "Rube" Foltz Family
& Edna Summey's New Ford V-8

The Reuben Foltz and the Cecil Woodworth families lived on adjoining farms for some 17 years. You get pretty well-acquainted and do a considerable amount of neighboring in that many years. Our families were no exception. We borrowed from each other, traded threshing labor and farm tools, and had picnics together. We also attended the same church, that being Bethel, a Methodist church.

There were five boys and one girl in the Foltz family and four boys and two girl Woodworths. William "Bill," Edna, Reuben Jr., Grandville, Roy, and Byron were the Foltz children. Edythe "Edie," Mary, Lloyd, Charles, Wayne, and Ted were the Woodworth's. I'm Ted.

In addition to both families attending the same church, we all went to the same school. That was Green School, the one built by my Great Grandfather, James Green. We often walked to school together and spent a lot of time together once we got there.

I mentioned exchanging tools. I've got to tell you about the time, rather one of the times, when I embarrassed my dad. Foltz's had drilled their wheat earlier than we had the fall before, so their wheat was ready for harvest ahead of ours. However, something happened to their binder wheel. The big one. So they borrowed ours, since our wheat wasn't quite ready to cut. Mr. Foltz must have forgotten that he had it because, one day he asked me why Dad hadn't cut his wheat yet. I told him it was because he hadn't returned our binder wheel. Dad was real upset with me for saying anything about the wheel, but we got it back.

Foltz's farm always seemed to look more prosperous than ours. One reason was that they had more horses than we did. And then there was the fact that they kept a sizable herd of dairy cattle and a bunch of brood sows. There always were either a lot of pigs or a lot of shoats being fattened for market, depending on the time of year. And chickens? Hattie always had a big flock of hens.

The Foltz family were from good German background. They believed strongly in the work ethic. "Rube," as the Dad was known, seemed to be successful at directing his five boys energy to constructive pursuits. They worked on the farm willingly. It was good training because all of them retained an interest in farming for the rest of their lives.

Like most farms in the area, the Foltz farm had what Rube thought was more than its fair share of rocks. A stone boat was an indispensable piece of farming equipment and it still is. Jacob Yoder, the present owner, has to pick rocks every year. Only difference is, he calls them stones.

Wait a minute! Hold on! Why did we call this sled conveyance a "stoneboat" when Dad always said we were loading it with rocks? Wonder if it had anything to do with "rocking the boat?" I'd guess not. Anyway, ...

It intrigued me that their farm, along the west side of the lane, had two barns midway between the main farm buildings and the woods. Fair sized, too. They were for hay storage. Rube and his sons raised a considerable amount of both alfalfa and red clover. Indiana weather requires hay to be stored inside, so barn storage was essential.

The main barn, up by the road and near the house, was in need of so much repair that Rube and the boys tore it down. In place of it, they had built the biggest, most impressive, bank barn that part of the country had ever seen. It was huge!

But, times change. Now, the two barns that stood alongside the lane are gone and Jacob Yoder has built on to the big barn. Now, it's really huge.

Mrs. Rube Foltz, Hattie, was one of my favorite people when I was a boy. She probably fed me more sugar cookies and hot cocoa than did my own mother. I'll never forget her. One of a kind.

While I'm thinking about it, it must have been about 1932 when Reuben Jr. went away to Divinity School and came back a full fledge, ordained, Methodist preacher. I can't recall that he ever had his own pulpit, but he did have the credentials. H-m-m-m-m,

"Reverend" Reuben Foltz Jr. I hadn't thought about that in a long time.

I don't remember the Foltz family ever owning a Model T Ford. I'm just sure they had bigger cars, like a Dodge-or maybe a Nash. Those were big cars compared to a Model T Ford. Bill, the oldest Foltz boy, married one of the daughters of William Sherman Kems. At about the same time, Edna, the only Foltz girl, married Dale Summey. A year or so later they had a son that they named David. Dale worked at the paper mill in White Pigeon, Michigan.

We'd heard about it but had not seen it. Edna's new car, that is. A brand, spanking new, Ford V-8. Then, one Sunday morning, there it was! Edna was driving into the church yard right past our kitchen window. I could not only see it but I could hear it. Now, I've heard of loud cars but that's not what I'm talking about here. It was a beautiful color. Jet black! A red pin stripe ran all the way around it just above the door handles. The air vents on the sides of the hood had up and down red stripes. And, the wire wheels were red.

Yes! Wire wheels! Virtually all cars, up 'til that time, had either wooden spoke wheels or disc metal wheels. I thought wire wheels were absolutely beautiful! Especially, red ones!

And all the fancy doo-dads! Two rear view mirrors! One on the inside and another on the outside. A pair of shiny chrome horns, just under the head lights, and a windshield wiper. The hood ornament was a greyhound dog and, to top everything off, wide, white sidewall tires!

I questioned Dad about the squeaking sound we heard as Edna drove up the kind of bumpy driveway. The sound was not unlike that of a bunch of excited mice.

"All new cars, like all new shoes, squeak. That's how you can tell they're new." Again, Dad had the answer.

Dad was good at helping me solve the deep mysteries of life.

47

Doing it-the Old Fashioned Way

Recently, my wife has been complaining about the price of soap. "It's too bad we can't make our own soap like my mama used to when I was a girl. But then, we never butcher a hog, do we?" Butchering a hog was a prerequisite to making soap.

Zena has an attack of nostalgia from time to time. I'm just sure she wouldn't really rather suffer the rigors of making soap the old fashioned way than enjoying the ease of buying it from the Super Market. But here is the way she tells about the "good old days":

"We ate a lot of bacon and ham on the farm. Mama always 'put down' the pork chops and sausage in big crocks. There were ten of us, altogether, so we ate a considerable amount of pork. That meant regular butchering resulting in numerous five gallon cans of lard. Even though we loved to eat them, there were more cracklings than we could consume. The lard and cracklings were the main ingredients in Mama's soap making. Sometimes she even made the lye that helped make the soap, from wood ashes. Mostly, though, she bought cans of lye from the store in Lebanon.

"It took all day and Mama worked from sun up to sundown on the day she made soap.

"The big, black, cast iron, kettle was suspended by an iron rod through the bail. Beneath it was plenty of room to build a wood fire that we kids kept feeding all day. It was important to keep the soap cooking.

"We made white soap for washing the dishes by using nothing but lard in the soap. The brown soap, for washing clothes, was a mixture of lard, cracklings, and meat drippings. Both kinds were harsh and hard on your hands.

"When the soap began to thicken, Mama would ladle it out in big flat pans and set it level on the porch. Just before it completely cooled and hardened, Mama would cut it in bar-sized pieces.

"Remembering back, I guess I didn't like it all that much. Making soap, I mean. I just appreciate the remembering."

Zena enjoys reminiscing. I couldn't help saying, "That reminds me of something I watched when I was a boy, nine years old. Fannie Shrock used to make her own soap."

"I'm not surprised. Everything reminds you of a story." She sounded a trifle irritated. "You might as well go ahead and tell me about it."

"Actually," I said, "she did it almost exactly the same way your mother did. Fannie called it lye soap and made it from cracklings, old lard, and grease. Ed Shrock used to save wood ashes from their stove and from these ashes they made their own lye. Ed put the ashes in a big trough under the eaves of a small tool shed. When it rained, the rain water would run off the roof and into the trough and then drain into a big crock at one end. Instant lye!"

The home manufacture of lye soap was only one of the ingenious methods farm wives had to make good use of something they had a surplus of. Most all farmers had a surplus of lard. Children generally felt that using hot grease to bake cake donuts was a fine method of getting rid of some of the abundance. I know I did.

Dad always liked sweet corn, so he raised more sweet corn than we could eat as roasting ears. Mom often cut the corn off the cob so she could serve just corn, maybe with milk, seasoned with salt and pepper. She also made a delicious corn casserole, often with some sausage in it. Mom also dried corn that she had cut off the cob. She had a huge pan. It must have been three feet square. It was made kind of like a double boiler so that she could put water in the bottom of it. The pan just about covered the whole top of the old cook stove. She'd spread the corn about a half inch deep in the top half of the pan. It took a lot of corn. The water in the bottom was kept hot and Mom seemed to stir and move the corn almost constantly until it was completely dried.

I can't remember how long it took to dry a can of sweet corn but I'm sure it was finished in one day. I do remember thinking that she didn't wind up with very much dried corn for her efforts. She was always back at it the next morning—and the next— because there was a surplus of corn. Everybody appreciated the dried corn in the winter, especially Mom's baked, dried, corn.

The sweet corn that my Dad and my brothers neglected to pick didn't go to waste. After the ears had dried some on the stalk, Dad would husk them part way. He'd tie up the small amount of husk left on the ear and hang the ears in the basement so they'd dry completely. In the winter, when Mom popped popcorn, she'd shell one of those ears of sweet corn and add it to the popcorn just before popping it. The end result was swollen, crunchy, kernels of corn. Dad said it was what the Indians called parched corn. I always considered it an extra special treat.

Fannie Shrock dried corn, too, with a lot of help from the children. Her method was quite different from my mother's way of doing it. She considered Mom's double boiler a down right modem convenience.

From my secret hiding place on top of our barn I used to watch the Shrock family dry corn the really old-fashioned way. Mrs. Shrock had some big pans, but they didn't have water in the bottom of them. Nor, did she put the pans on the stove. What she did was put the pans on the roof of the little tool shed on the side facing the sun. Then, two of the Shrock children, one on each end of the roof, would sit all day long chasing the flies away with limbs from the peach tree, and stirring the corn. It took several days for the sun to dry the corn, but eventually it did.

Mom never dried anything but corn. Not so, the Shrocks. After the corn crop was finished, there were apples and peaches to dry. I know it wasn't the case but it seemed as though Alma and Martha, or Paul and Petey, or Paul and Silas, spent the whole summer on that roof chasing flies away with a peach tree limb.

One thing I do know, as winter time set in, the Shrocks had a basement bulging with potatoes, acorn squash, beets, and turnips. Also, There was dried corn, dried beans and dried fruit. It would have taken a mathematician to count all the jars of canned fruit and vegetables. For instance, enough green beans and tomatoes to feed an army.

Ed Shrock read the Bible a lot. He taught his family that "God helps him who helps himself." He also believed in the idea of, "Waste not. Want not." They were a fine family, the Shrocks.

176

The Lost Dime

48

There are those who say, "Truth is stranger than fiction." Others are wont to exclaim, "I don't believe it" even when hearing the truth. Sometimes the truth is hard to accept if the circumstances being described are something we personally have not experienced.

Very probably many of the experiences I had as a child were eventually beneficial to me. But, it took a long time for me to see how that could be. One Wednesday night, in late summer of the year 1931, Dad took me to town with him. It was an opportunity for me to play, or associate with, other children. Wednesday night was Band Concert Night and lots of people came into LaGrange to enjoy the music and to shop.

During the course of the evening, I noted that some of the boys I'd gotten acquainted with were sucking on "all day" suckers. Naturally, I didn't have any money and I felt kind of left out. One of the boys said, "Why don't you ask your Dad for a penny?"

Admittedly, I wouldn't have done it on my own but the boys goaded me into it. I went into Fisher's Cigar Store where Dad was playing cards.

"Dad, can I have a penny for an 'all day' sucker?"

The men playing cards with Dad looked up to see what Dads reaction would be. "Sure thing, Ted." With that he took out his pocket book, unsnapped the coin purse, and selected a penny for me. I'm virtually positive he wouldn't have given me the penny had it not been for the fact that his cronies were watching.

I bought the candy at the 5 and 10 cent store. The reason it was called an "all day" sucker was that it lasted nearly that long if you just sucked on it. The thing was as big as a golf ball and was

177

definitely a mouth full. That was the only time I can remember Dad ever having given me a penny.

Earlier, I mentioned my friend John, the Catholic, who lived at the County Farm. He gave me a Buffalo nickel. To the very best of my recollection, that's all the money I had ever had-six cents. My next experience with money took place in the spring of 1932. Now, if you can stand it, I'm going to tell you another story about shearing sheep. This time it involved the Presdorf family.

Loren Presdorf's farm was only about a mile and a half from the parsonage where Dad and I lived. I generally was able to find a reason for being glad to be with my father.

Maybe that's all it was, the fact I was with him. Shearing sheep can hardly be classified as fun so it must have been something else. If Dad's back wasn't hurting he was reasonably good company.

It was Friday and Dad wanted to get started early so we could finish Loren's flock in one day. That way, we could do Bill Presdorf's on a Saturday when his children were home from school. They liked to not only watch the shearing process but willingly helped in any way they could. It's just a small blip in my memory but I have an incredible picture in my mind of something that happened the morning we were at Loren's.

Since we lived so close by we got to his farm early. He hadn't yet finished his chores and so had not penned up the sheep. They still had to be rounded up from the pasture and be brought to the barn.

Although it wasn't a cold day, it was windy. Once we had all the sheep pretty well together we started driving them toward the barn. That's when the incident occurred that is so well-etched in my memory. Loren stopped to roll a cigarette.

Remember, now, those were depression days and a pack of the least expensive cigarettes cost ten cents for a pack of 20 or three packs for $0.25. However, a sack of Bull Durham or Duke's Mixture tobacco only cost five cents. One who had developed a knack for it could roll twice as many cigarettes from either kind of tobacco as there were in one "store-bought" package.

First, Loren took a paper from the pack of thin cigarette papers. Then he loosened the draw string on the tobacco sack. Holding the paper in his left hand in such a way as to form a sort of trench shape he tapped some tobacco into it with his right hand. Before he could get the bag to his mouth, so he could grasp the paper tab in his teeth and tighten the draw string, the wind blew the tobacco out of the cigarette paper.

One more time he spilled the brown flecks of tobacco onto the paper. One more time a gust of wind blew it away. Throwing the paper down in disgust, Loren walked toward the flock of sheep as they headed toward the barn. And that's the picture of Loren Presdorf I've carried in my head all these years.

The next day was Saturday and we were at Bill Presdorf's farm. Early. They were ready for us. The sheep were penned in the barn and they had prepared an area for us to use to shear the sheep. A heavy layer of straw had been spread on the floor and Bill had brought out a tarp, about 12 foot square, and had laid it on top of the straw.

We got started right away. Dad was feeling good, partly, because we'd had smooth sailing the day before. Once we got the sheep in the barn, that's it. I felt good, too, because there were several Presdorf children. Don was the oldest, then Bernice. Robert was a year ahead of me in school so was most likely only a year older.

Hold on! I nearly forgot what I wanted to write about! After we finished shearing Loren's 22 sheep, Loren paid Dad $2.20 or ten cents a head. He paid with two one dollar bills and two dimes. And guess what? Dad said, "Ted, you worked real hard today and I'm going to reward you."

With that, he handed me one of the dimes. "Here, this is for you. It's a lot of money. Take care of it."

"Oh, I will! I will! Thank you!" I thought I was rich. At that moment I really loved my father.

The next day, while in Bill Presdorf's barn, I must have taken that dime out of my pocket a hundred times. Enough times to punch a hole in my pocket. Then, catastrophe! I lost the dime!

"Dad! Dad! I've lost the dime! There's a hole in my pocket and I lost the dime you gave me!" I'd never been so unhappy.

Dad wasn't happy either. Far from it. I was scared half to death worrying about what he'd do to punish me if we couldn't find it.

We searched the straw for what seemed like an hour. All of us. The Presdorf's, too. No success. We didn't find it. It had been like trying to find the proverbial needle in a haystack.

The punishment was very simple and straightforward:

Dad looked grimly at me and said, "I declare, Teddy boy! It's obvious to me that you just don't know how to take care of money. Well, I'm going to put a quietus to that. I promise you, I'll never, ever, give you any money again!"

My father was a man of his word. I was 56 years old when he died at the age of 93. In all those years he never, ever, gave me any more money. You know something? He just very well might have done me a tremendous favor.

49

May I Sleep in Your Barn Tonight, Mister?

"There he is, again!" My wife was pointing to a pan handler standing on the curb of the esplanade in the busy intersection.

We were, in fact, nearly stalled in traffic because of some construction work up ahead. The traffic signal was letting about three cars pass through each time the light was green. This gave us plenty of time to observe—and make a comment on—the man with the card.

No Job—No Money— Hungry—Help Me—God Bless You." The message was written in five lines in black on a piece of cardboard about 18 inches square. He's there with the sign almost every time we pass through the intersection. I guess it's his corner.

"Slim," as we've dubbed him, is nearly six feet tall and very slim. No! He's actually down right skinny! It's likely he doesn't weigh more.than 100 pounds, soaking wet. And I've seen him that way, too.

For a fact, "Slim" always looks hungry and it's very possible he doesn't get enough to eat. One thing for sure, he gets enough to drink. You can smell the alcohol even with your car windows closed.

The real "draw" is his aluminum crutch. He kind of leans on this crutch as he walks alongside the cars showing the occupants his sign. The crutch, along with his decrepit clothes and unshaven face, gives him a pathetic look. It works, too, because almost every other motorist handed a bill to him. He bowed to them and stuffed the dollar, or whatever, into his pants pocket.

Minimum—Minimum! I saw five people hand him paper money in a span of some two or three minutes. Well, needless to say, I didn't contribute. The way I looked at it, he was making

181

money faster than I ever had in my entire life. I believe in helping those who are in need, but I didn't feel that he qualified.

Zena began reminiscing, again. This time about the contrast between men like "Slim" and those she'd met who were out of work during the Great Depression. She, and her family, had lived on a farm in Kansas. The road they lived on, U.S. 281, ran between Red Cloud, Nebraska and Great Bend, Kansas—and beyond, in both directions.

At least once a month, and more often during the summer, one of these out of work men would stop by their farm. Zena remembered them as usually carrying a bag or some kind of satchel.

"'Could you spare a hungry man a bite to eat, Ma'am? I'd be glad to split some wood or do whatever needs doin'.'

"They were always polite and respectful as well as thin and hungry.

"Mom never asked them to do any work, but she always gave them a big, thick, slice of homemade bread spread liberally with fresh churned butter. Oh, yes! And a big glass of milk. While he'd sit on the front porch, eating, we'd ask him questions about where he'd been and where he was going. They always talked to us and answered our questions.

"Most of them had families back home and they wanted to talk and show us pictures. It was kind of sad, the stories they'd tell.

"Some people called them bums or hoboes, but they were just unfortunate men looking for work. We never had any fear or distrust of them. They never tried to steal from us or do us any harm. I just felt real sorry for them."

"My sentiments, exactly!" I told her.

Actually, while we lived at the parsonage, I don't remember even one of them stopping at our house. They always stopped at the Shrocks. Ed and Fannie Shrock never turned a hungry person away.

Some while back I was trying to remember a song that must have been well known during the depression years. Well, sir, I got a lot of help from my friends. About a dozen of them.

Sung to the tune of "Red River Valley," it was my brother Wayne's favorite "Somebody done somebody wrong songs."

Here it is:

182

May I Sleep In your Barn Tonight, Mister?

I

One night it was cold dark and stormy
When along came a tramp in the rain
He was making his way to some station
To catch a long distance train.

II

May I sleep in your barn tonight, Mister?
For it's cold lying out on the ground
The cold north wind is a whistling
And I have no place to lie down.

III

Oh, I have no tobacco or matches
And I'm sure that I'll do you no harm
Let me tell you my story, kind Mister
For it runs through my heart like a storm.

IV

It was three years ago last summer
I shall never forget that sad day
When a stranger came out from the city
And said that he wanted to stay.

V

Now my wife said she'd like to be earning
Some more money to add to our home
And so it was finally decided
That the stranger might stay at our home.

VI

One night as I came from my workshop
I was whistling and singing with joy
I expected a kind hearted welcome
From my sweet loving wife and my boy.

VII

When what should find but a letter
They had placed it right there on the stand
The moment my eyes fell upon it
I picked it right up in my hand

VIII
Now this note said my wife and this stranger
Had left and had taken our son
Oh, I wonder how God up in heaven
Will reward what the stranger has done!

Now, isn't that a real tear jerker?

Glada Holst, I think it was, made a substitution for verse number five. It goes:

Now the man he was fair tall and handsome
And he looked like a man who had wealth
And he wanted to stay in the country
Said he needed to stay for his health.

That sounds all right. Maybe it could be added between verses five and six. Sylvia Hostetler was the one who sent me the complete song. Mrs. Hostetler was born and raised on a farm and spent her whole life there. Sheltered from the world, you might say.

Her comment about the song was:

"Very sad! But I guess things like that happen. It's a good thing I don't know the many sad things that are happening in this world. I could hardly take it. But, God sees it all and these folks will be punished."

She's right, you know.

50

Evicted Again

Dad opened the letter and almost as soon as he commenced to read it his face began getting redder and redder. He was soon what is called "livid" with anger. Dad had a real bad temper and when he lost it, it was a good idea to stay out of his way until he cooled off. This time, it took a while.

We'd lived in the parsonage of the Bethel Church for almost exactly a year, now. I had just turned nine when we moved in and now I was just past ten. I had attended Saylor School all of the fourth grade and had learned some very good lessons from Miss Elizabeth Neely. She was a fairly typical one room school teacher. Heavy on psychology. I was reminded of her a good many years later while I was in the Army. As a private, I was resisting an order given me by a Sergeant. His final comment was, "You're absolutely right! I can't make you do it. But, I can sure make you wish you would have!"

The eight months I spent at Saylor School left me with many memories—mostly good ones.

Spelling bee's were a highlight for me. The fourth grade was probably my best year in spelling, thanks, in great measure, to Miss Neely. She also helped me to better understand arithmetic.

I felt as though I was an outsider at first, but it didn't last. I made a host of friends. Paul and Alma Shrock were probably my closest friends. We spent a good deal of time together away from school, too. Surely, I'll never forget their dog, Rover. The name was appropriate for he did rove form time to time.

Never could I think of Saylor School without a flash back of Art Kerns and his wicked left handed pitching. His sisters, Evelyn and Marcella, are in my memory bank, too.

Bruce and Thelma Slack, June and Chuck Parsons, Jim and Chester Rigsby, Troyers, and many more—they became friends of mine at Saylor.

I had known the Eaton family since I was a wee lad. Living so close by, I really got to know Merril and Vera as well as their boys, Robert, Glendon, and Daryle. More than once I had been privileged to eat Vera's delicious cooking. Turning the crank to run the sheep shearing rig for Dad wasn't what I'd call fun, but I'll never forget the dinners we had. The farm wives went all out to cook us a good meal and I didn't soon forget them.

Cecil Christler's geese! To this day it makes me uneasy when I hear a gander's his-s-s-s! I prefer my geese flying in their "V" formation high overhead.

Would I soon forget Beatty Hostetler or his motorcycles? Of course not! Anyway, I was going to have a good many more experiences involving him in the next few years.

My excursions with Beatty Hostetler have been among my most exciting memories.

My brother, Lloyd, and riding the western horse to Shipshewana was one of the stand out memories of my year at Saylor. I got to watch him break that particular bucking bronco. Carl Dintaman said Lloyd broke one for his dad that was worse yet. I believe Lloyd would have tried anything, once, so long as it wasn't either illegal or immoral. Now that I think of it, he used to pass up anything that was fattening, too.

I enjoyed the trips to visit Mom at the County Infirmary. I'll never forget the conversations I had with Uncle Austin, Little John, and Pete the Berry Picker. Those men helped further my education immeasurably by answering my many questions.

And then there was John, the first Catholic I had ever met. I thought John was fat, but probably he was just big. He wasn't actually rich, just generous. But for a fact, he did have a wooden leg. So you see how a nine year old boy got his first impression of a Catholic.

Visits from Mary and Truman, sister Edie's Shivaree, baseball on Sunday afternoon, singing by myself in the church—when it was empty, nights spent at the Shrocks—all were beautiful memories of the year I was nine.

Back to the letter.

Dad had cooled down, or at least lowered his voice, when I came back into the house. "When does school start, Ted?"

"The day after Labor Day and that's next week. You're supposed to try to get me some new school clothes. Don't you remember?"

"There won't be any new clothes. Maybe you can get some "hand me downs" from John Doney. I don't even have enough money to pay the rent. That's what the letter was about."

"Are we going to have to move?" I was worried.

"That was the gist of the letter!"

"Who was it from, Pa?"

"It was signed by George Grantham, the preacher, but you can just bet that bunch of parsimonious old Biddies that try to run the church put him up to it. The whole lot of 'em aren't worth a picayune but that don't stop 'em from attacking me when I'm down!"

Dad didn't go to church himself and considered most who did to be hypocrites. He wasn't bashful about saying as much, either.

"Where will we move to?" I wanted to know.

"Don't know yet, but I'll work on it tomorrow. In the meantime, you get a good night's sleep. When you get around to it in the morning I want you to pick all the acorn squash and put them in gunny sacks. Pick all the tomatoes that have any size at all. Put the pink and red ones in separate baskets from the green ones. Whatever else you find we can use—pick it. We'll take everything with us that we can. The potatoes are already dug and in the basement. They'll have to be sacked up, too."

With that, we went to bed.

Dad left early the next morning. Soon thereafter, I was out in the garden. The assignment made me feel important. There weren't as many squash as I had hoped. I did get a lot of tomatoes, mostly green, as well as beets and carrots. That weekend we moved in with Grandma Woodworth.

Without any money, Dad wasn't able to find a place to rent.

As I found out later, Dad hadn't paid the rent for the past three months. At $3.00 per month, we owed a total of $9.00 or move

187

out. So, we moved out because we couldn't afford to pay $3.00 a month rent.

Evicted! Again!"

Pastor George Grantham and his wife, Barbara

www.ingramcontent.com/pod-product-compliance
Lightning Source LLC
Chambersburg PA
CBHW060850280326
41934CB00007B/995